OSPREY AIRCRAFT OF THE ACES • 90

Fiat CR.42 Aces of World War 2

85 2
3

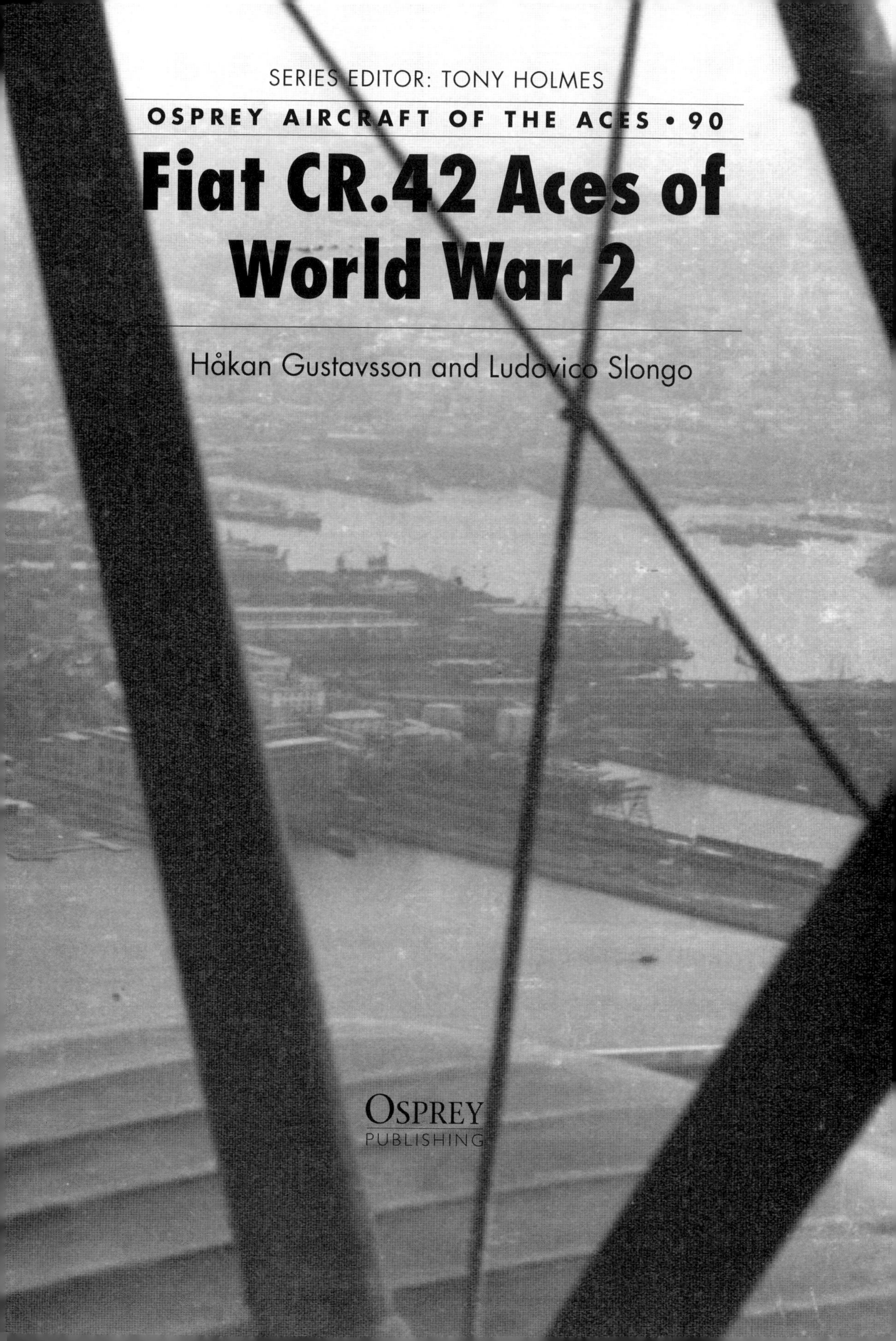

SERIES EDITOR: TONY HOLMES

OSPREY AIRCRAFT OF THE ACES • 90

Fiat CR.42 Aces of World War 2

Håkan Gustavsson and Ludovico Slongo

OSPREY
PUBLISHING

Front cover
On the morning of 6 November 1940, the first British offensive of World War 2 was launched when troops in Sudan invaded neighbouring Abyssinia in an effort to capture the Italian border fort at Gallabat and occupy nearby Metemma. Three Gladiator Is of No 112 Sqn's 'K' Flight were tasked with providing air cover for the advancing troops, and as they were patrolling at low-level to the east of Metemma, a formation of eight CR.42s from 412ª *Squadriglia*, led by unit commander Capitano Antonio Raffi, attacked them from out of the sun. The Gladiator pilots were taken by surprise, and 24-year-old Flt Lt Kenneth Howard Savage, in Gladiator I L7614, was killed, while Plt Off Kirk (K7969) was forced to take to his parachute – neither pilot had seen their attacker. Plt Off Jack Hamlyn evaded the initial onslaught, but his aircraft (L7612) was so badly damaged that he had to force-land. Hamlyn subsequently returned to base on foot.

This one-sided engagement had brought 412ª *Squadriglia* the first of its six victories on this date, two of which were credited to Tenente Mario Visintini as his ninth and tenth kills. By the time of his death in a flying accident on 11 February 1941, Visintini had become the most successful biplane fighter ace of World War 2, with 16 and 2 shared victories to his name in the CR.42 – he also had an additional kill that he had claimed while flying a CR.32 with Nationalist forces in the Spanish Civil War (*Cover artwork by Mark Postlethwaite*)

First published in Great Britain in 2009 by Osprey Publishing
Midland House, West Way, Botley, Oxford, OX2 0PH
443 Park Avenue South, New York, NY, 10016, USA
E-mail: info@ospreypublishing.com

ISBN 13: 978 1 84603 427 5

Edited by Tony Holmes and Bruce Hales-Dutton
Page design by Tony Truscott
Cover Artwork by Mark Postlethwaite
Aircraft Profiles by Richard Caruana
Scale Drawings by Mark Styling
Index by Alan Thatcher
Originated by PDQ Digital Media Solutions, UK
Printed and bound in China by Bookbuilders

09 10 11 12 13 14 10 9 8 7 6 5 4 3 2 1

Acknowledgements
This book is the end result of many years of research, and the authors would like to thank the following individuals for help, inspiration and encouragement during this period – Csaba Becse, Ferdinando D'Amico, Nick Beale, Fulvio Chianese, Nicola Malizia, Giovanni Massimello, Sergio Santoro, Giandrea Bussi, Giorgio Apostolo, Manlio Palmieri, Michele M Gaetani, Bruno Dilecce, Enrico Locatelli, Enrico Leproni, Marco Gargari, Luca Delle Canne, Gabriele Brancaccio, Renato Zavattini, Roger Juglair, Andrea Fabianelli, Dénes Bernád, Roberto Gentilli, Michele Palermo, Enrico Cernuschi and Peter Taghon.

CONTENTS

INTRODUCTION

On the afternoon of 27 October 1942, a formation of 16 American P-40F Warhawks from the USAAF's 57th Fighter Group was on its way to attack Axis troops and vehicles over the El Alamein line when the American pilots discovered a huge formation of enemy aircraft. In front of them, formed up as if for an air display, were 20 Fiat CR.42 biplanes. Nearby was a similar number of Luftwaffe Ju 87 Stuka dive-bombers escorted by 18 Bf 109Fs. The American pilots attacked, later claiming to have downed four CR.42s. Three more were listed as probables, plus three damaged, and there were no American losses. Lt Roy Whittaker, who later became one of the top-scoring P-40 pilots in-theatre, claimed a victory during the combat.

That afternoon the American pilots had taken part in a more significant action than they realised. In one of the last desperate attempts to save the day for the Axis forces at El Alamein, General Erwin Rommel had planned a counter-attack in the northern sector of the front. Having decided to commit most of his surviving armoured forces, he had personally requested a maximum effort from Axis air power in an attempt to destroy artillery emplacements in the Tell el Eisa area that had previously played a critical role in repulsing his panzers.

For this very reason, all available Italian assault aircraft – no fewer than 43 CR.42s (30 from the *gruppi* of 50° *Stormo* and 13 from 101° *Gruppo Autonomo*) had taken off at 1400 hrs. Macchi C.202 fighters from

A lone CR.42 flies over Rome, the 'Eternal City', shortly before Italy entered World War 2 in June 1940. At lower left is the St Peter's Basilica, and St Peter's Square can also be seen (*Roberto Gentilli*)

3° and 4° *Stormi* covered the formation's left flank, while to the right were the Ju 87s escorted by 18 Bf 109Fs of JG 27. The CO of 50° *Stormo,* Tenente Colonello Ferruccio Vosilla, was leading his men, the unit's fighter-bomber CR.42s having recently been removed from frontline daylight operations because of their vulnerability to enemy fighters. However, the severity of the situation on the ground was such that the risk of using them now seemed justified.

The Italian formation, led by the 50° *Stormo* biplanes flying in vics disposed in echelon right, encountered Allied fighters, said to be 'around 70 Curtiss, some with American insignia', over the target. They immediately drew the attention of the escort, leaving the Fiat biplanes unprotected. Suddenly, more P-40s appeared, diving on the CR.42s from above. Apart from the USAAF Warhawks, the Axis formation was also intercepted by 24 RAF Hurricane IIs of Nos 213 and 33 Sqns and at least four Spitfire VCs of No 601 Sqn. Vosilla, who had already started his attack run when the fighters appeared, jettisoned his bombs and made a climbing turn to face the enemy interceptors head-on.

The bombing mission became totally disorganised, and a confused melee ensued. When it was over, five CR.42s, piloted by Sergente Maggiore Umberto Suzzi of 101° *Gruppo* and Capitano Giordano Bruno Rossoni, Tenente Pietro Vodret, Sottotenente Mario Aimi and Sergente Maggiore Costante Cipitelli of 50° *Stormo* had all been shot down by the P-40s. No 213 Sqn claimed an additional CR.42 and two probables. All the pilots apart from Suzzi were able to force-land and subsequently return to their base. Tenente Vodret and Sottotenente Francesco Iadanza each claimed to have shot down a P-40. It is possible, however, that they had shot down the No 213 Sqn Hurricane II of Flt Sgt S G Brooks. This was Iadanza's second kill, as he had previously claimed another P-40 (actually the No 73 Sqn Hurricane II of Flt Lt John Beauchamp Selby) on 10 July 1942.

Once back at base, Vosilla stated that his men had hit the target, although reports from 101° *Gruppo's* pilots suggest that this was not the case. Vosilla's evasive manoeuvre had, however, saved his vulnerable biplanes from suffering far higher losses. That day at El Alamein the CR.42s had performed their last important mission over the frontline. In doing so they had clearly demonstrated that, at the end of 1942, they were now quite unsuited to this kind of operation. Accordingly, they were rapidly relegated to second-line duties within the *Regia Aeronautica.*

VETERAN PILOT

At 37, Feruccio Vosilla was a very popular leader amongst his men. His quick manoeuvring when faced by enemy fighters revealed just how experienced a pilot he was by October 1942. Indeed, Vosilla had first seen aerial action as long ago as 1929, when he flew missions during the conflict in Libya. More combat followed in East Africa in 1935-36 and during the Spanish Civil War. By 1942 Vosilla had been flying the CR.42 for three years, and had claimed several victories on the type.

He had first flown the Fiat biplane against enemy aircraft on 15 June 1940 when, as CO of 18° *Gruppo,* he led 15 aircraft supporting the CR.42s of 23° and 150° *Gruppi* in an attack on the French airfields of Le Cannet des Maures and Cuers Pierrefeu, in Provence. An hour after

take-off, and at an altitude of 18,000 ft, he and his pilots were surprised by enemy fighters that suddenly appeared from a cloudbank. The newcomers were identified as Morane-Saulnier MS.406s and another type not positively identified. In the ensuing combat the Italians claimed to have shot down three French fighrters, and the victories were shared between all 15 pilots. Two CR.42s from 83ª *Squadriglia* were lost in return, with one pilot killed and the other captured.

Meanwhile, the 150° *Gruppo* formation was completing its strafing attack of Cuers Pierrefeu, where it had destroyed at least six Vought 156s of *Escadrille de Bombardement en Piquè* AB3 on the ground. Five Bloch MB 151s of *Escadrille de Chasse* AC3 had also been shot down shortly after they had been bounced immediately after take-off. However, the *gruppo* lost adjutant Capitano Nino Caselli, and another aircraft encountered mechanical trouble and force-landed in enemy territory.

At Le Cannet des Maures, 23° *Gruppo* strafed the airstrip and destroyed at least three Dewoitine D.520s on the ground. But here too the Italian pilots reported being surprised by 'four or five Moranes and Dewoitines'. The French fighters shot down 75ª *Squadriglia* CO, Capitano Luigi Filippi, who was taken prisoner. Three of the five Italian losses on this date had been caused by French ace Sous Lt Pierre Le Gloan of the *5eme Escadrille* of GC III/6. An outstanding pilot who would end the conflict with 18 kills to his credit, Le Gloan had been flying a D.520.

These battles have come to be regarded as clear proof of the all-round inferiority of the Fiat biplane when opposed by modern monoplanes such as the MS.406 and D.520. In reality, the CR.42 pilots had made a relatively successful series of ground attack missions and shot down at least as many enemy fighters as they had lost. Moreover, the Italian pilots had demonstrated that when not the victims of 'hit and run' tactics, which saw monoplane fighters bouncing them from above at great speeds, they could hold their own in combat even against more modern fighters. This would be confirmed by the events of the months to come.

The fact that a biplane fighter with fixed landing gear and an open cockpit was still in service with a nation then reputed to have a powerful air force was not so strange in 1940. In fact Italy was not alone in

Maggiore Ferruccio Vosilla, CO of 18° *Gruppo*, claimed three shared victories during the short French campaign. Here, he stands in front of his partially camouflaged aircraft at Vilanova in June 1940. A white band was added to the rear fuselage of the aircraft shortly after this photograph was taken. The *gruppo* CO's pennant can clearly be seen to the left of Vosilla (*Giuseppe Ruzzin via Giandrea Bussi*)

numbering biplanes among its frontline units. Other great powers to do so were Great Britain, which had six squadrons of Gloster Gladiators, and the Soviet Union, whose air force was still equipped with Polikarpov I-153s.

Peculiar to Italy, however, was the fact that its biplanes were not old machines close to retirement. Instead, the CR.42 represented one of the most modern types then available, and many units were still waiting to receive them. Italy's desire to cling onto biplane types when all other countries were switching to monoplanes has been variously explained as a mix of conservative thinking by the *Regia Aeronautica,* reinforced by the success recently achieved by the *Falco's* predecessor, the CR.32, during the Spanish Civil War. The type's manoeuvrability was another factor, demanded by pilots and considered to form the basis of most air combat tactics. Finally, the economic influence exerted by the Fiat group may have been a factor in the adoption of its new product by the air force.

Seen here dressed in his flying overalls, hands in pockets, at Mirafiori (east of the Franco-Italian border) in June 1940, Maresciallo Felice Longhi claimed one and three shared victories in the CR.42 while serving with 18° *Gruppo*. This particular aircraft was his personal mount during 1940-41, and he used it to down a Blenheim in North Africa. Longhi had previously scored a single victory flying a CR.32 in Spain. His tally stood at six and four shared kills by war's end (*via Giorgio Apostolo*)

Whatever the reasons, the CR.42, although absolutely not up to the best European fighters of its time like the D.520, Spitfire or Bf 109, was still considered a relatively adequate war machine in the summer of 1940. Very fast for a biplane (it had a top speed of 267 mph), and retaining the specific characteristics of the type such as manoeuvrability, good handling and a high rate of climb, the *Falco's* main weaknesses lay in its equipment.

The fighter was armed with just a pair of Breda SAFAT machine guns, often of different calibres – one of 12.7 mm and one of 7.7 mm. This represented a step backwards even when compared to the CR.32, in which both guns were of 12.7 mm calibre. Moreover, the weapons were synchronised to fire through the propeller arc, resulting in a low rate of fire and many difficulties in maintaining the complex synchronising mechanism in the field. The *Falco* also lacked any kind of armour protection for its pilot, boasted only basic cockpit instrumentation that did not help flight in bad weather or at night, and had no radio equipment – the first sets were tested in late 1940, but without success.

Yet despite these shortcomings, the CR.42 remained able to fight on equal terms with most of the aircraft opposing it in the Mediterranean theatre up until mid-1941. With the passing of time, however, its inadequacy became all too clear, although it remained in active service until war's end. But this was chiefly because the Italian aircraft industry failed to supply modern replacements in sufficient numbers.

A CR.42 from 2° *Stormo's* 95ª *Squadriglia* is seen on the wing in North Africa in early 1941. Although outclassed by Allied fighters in-theatre by this stage of the conflict, *Falcos* from the unit still enjoyed occasional successes against Blenheims and Wellingtons that were targeting Axis shipping convoys in the Mediterranean (*via Giorgio Apostolo*)

OPENING BATTLES

When Italy declared war on Britain and France on 10 June 1940, some 300 CR.42s equipped roughly half of the *Regia Aeronautica's* fighter units. Of this number, around 220 aircraft were combat-ready. In northwest Italy, II^a *Divisione Aerea 'Borea'* was the formation tasked with mounting attacks on France. Its fighter units, assigned to I^a *Squadra Aerea,* were comprised of;

53° *Stormo* (Colonello Arrigo Tessari)
150° *Gruppo* (Tenente Colonello Rolando Pratelli)
363^a *Squadriglia* (Capitano Luigi Mariotti)
364^a *Squadriglia* (Capitano Nicola Magaldi)
365^a *Squadriglia* (Capitano Giorgio Graffer)
151° Gruppo (Maggiore Carlo Calosso)
366^a *Squadriglia* (Capitano Bernardino Serafini)
367^a *Squadriglia* (Capitano Simeone Marsan)
368^a *Squadriglia* (Capitano Bruno Locatelli)

3° *Stormo* (Colonello Fortunato Rolando)
18° *Gruppo* (Maggiore Ferruccio Vosilla
83^a *Squadriglia* (Capitano Edoardo Molinari)
85^a *Squadriglia* (Capitano Giulio Anelli)
95^a *Squadriglia* (Capitano Gino Lodi)
23° *Gruppo* (Maggiore Tito Falconi)
70^a *Squadriglia* (Capitano Ottorino Fargnoli)
74^a *Squadriglia* (Capitano Guido Bobba)
75^a *Squadriglia* (Capitano Luigi Filippi)

Additionally, II^a *Squadra Aerea,* which had moved to Sicily, left 9° *Gruppo* of 4° *Stormo* in northeast Italy to guard the frontier with Yugoslavia. It comprised;

9° *Gruppo* (Maggiore Ernesto Botto)
73^a *Squadriglia* (Tenente Vittorio Pezzè)
96^a *Squadriglia* (Capitano Roberto Fassi)
97^a *Squadriglia* (Capitano Antonio Larsimont-Pergameni)

CR.42 MM4357 '85-3' of 85^a *Squadriglia,* 18° *Gruppo* is seen here on patrol at the very beginning of the war (*Giuseppe Ruzzin via Giandrea Bussi*)

In Sicily, as part of Iª *Divisione Aerea 'Aquila'*, the fighter units of IIª *Squadra Aerea* that was operating over the British fortress of Malta and against the French forces were;

157° *Gruppo* (Maggiore Guido Nobili)
384ª Squadriglia (Capitano Mario Frulla)
385ª *Squadriglia* (Capitano Aldo Li Greci)
386ª *Squadriglia* (Capitano Gustavo Garretto)

In Libya, part of *Aeronautica della Libia* (which was soon to become Vª *Squadra Aerea*), which was opposing the British forces based in Egypt there, included the partially CR.42-equipped 2° *Stormo*. It controlled the following units;

2° *Stormo*
10° *Gruppo* (Tenente Colonello Armando Piragino)
84ª *Squadriglia* (Capitano Luigi Monti)
90ª *Squadriglia* (Capitano Renzo Maggini)
91ª *Squadriglia* (Capitano Giuseppe D'Agostinis)
13° *Gruppo* (Maggiore Secondo Revetria)
77ª *Squadriglia* (Capitano Mario Fedele)
78ª *Squadriglia* (Capitano Giuseppe Dall'Aglio)
82ª *Squadriglia* (Capitano Guglielmo Arrabito)

CR.42 MM5024 '385-1' of Capitano Aldo Li Greci, CO of 385ª *Squadriglia*, 157° *Gruppo*, 1° *Stormo* heads a line up of *Falcos* at the Sicilian airfield of Trapani-Milo in July 1940 (*Casucci via Andrea Fabianelli*)

Sottotenente Michele Casucci poses for the photographer in front of the tail of his CR.42 MM5024 '385-5' of 385ª *Squadriglia*, 157° *Gruppo* again at Trapani-Milo in July 1940 (*Casucci via Andrea Fabianelli*)

An additional unit equipped with the CR.42 was based in Albania as part of *Aeronautica dell'Albania*, 160° *Gruppo Autonomo* (Tenente Colonello Raffaele Colacicchi) controlling 395ª *Squadriglia* (Capitano Pier Giuseppe Scarpetta). The remaining two *squadriglie* within the *Gruppo* were still flying CR.32s.

Finally, to reinforce the air force based in East Africa, the *Regia Aeronautica* had planned on sending a complete *gruppo* of CR.42s to the region. However, due to a shortage of aircraft, it had only been possible to despatch two *squadriglie* of biplanes (although at full strength) during the spring of 1940. 412ª (Capitano Antonio Raffi) had been formed with pilots drawn from 84ª *Squadriglia* of 4° *Stormo*, and 413ª (Capitano Corrado Santoro) had been established with pilots from 364ª *Squadriglia* of 53° *Stormo*. A third resident *squadriglia*, 414ª (Capitano Vincenzo Lucertini), had been partially equipped with CR.42s by June 1940. The units protected the bases of Massawa and Assab in the north of the country, as well as facing Commonwealth forces in Sudan and Aden.

Still more units were scheduled to replace their CR.32s with CR.42s, but the relatively low production rate at the Fiat works delayed this. Indeed, as the beginning of the war the plant's productive output was sufficient only to make good the increasing combat loss rate, hence the fact that 160° *Gruppo* was still largely equipped with the older Fiat fighter when war broke out in Greece in October. Libya-based 8° *Gruppo* replaced its CR.32s at the beginning of July, while that same month in Sicily, the elite 17° *Gruppo* of 1° *Stormo* had to temporarily revert back to the elderly Fiat biplane when deliveries of the new Macchi C.200 monoplane fighter were delayed. Finally, Sardinia-based 3° *Gruppo Autonomo* remained partially equipped with CR.32s well into 1941, as did the autonomous *squadriglie* based in Rhodes.

First blood

In Italian service, the *Falco* drew its first blood in the early afternoon of 12 June 1940 over Eritrea when a section of fighters from 412ª *Squadriglia* scrambled to intercept nine RAF Wellesleys of No 223 Sqn that had been sent to attack the airfield of Gura. Recently promoted Tenente Carlo Canella claimed to have shot down K7747, although this

A CR.42 of 77ª *Squadriglia*, 13° *Gruppo* has its engine run up at Tripoli Castel Benito, in Libya, during the summer of 1940. Note that the aircraft lacks a spinner, indicating that this photograph was taken while the fighter was being tested following maintenance. The *Squadriglia's* official badge – a red heart in a white disc – can be seen on the wheel spat. 13° *Gruppo* (77ª, 78ª and 82ª *Squadriglie*) was commanded by Maggiore Secondo Revetria and based at Tripoli Castel Benito airfield when the war started, the unit being equipped with 25 combat-ready CR.42s and 11 CR.32s. It was the only *gruppo* in Libya to operate CR.42s at this time (*Roberto Gentilli*)

CR.42s from 90ª *Squadriglia*, 10° *Gruppo*, 4° *Stormo CT* in North Africa. This shot is dominated by the *Squadriglia's* elephant war insignia. The photograph was taken after 12 June 1940, as two of the aircraft in the background display white rudder crosses – a marking applied at around this time. 90ª *Squadriglia* was commanded by Capitano Renzo Maggini in 1940, and the unit included future aces Franco Lucchini (21) Angelo Savini (7) and Amleto Monterumici (5) within its ranks (*Renato Zavattini*)

aircraft, heavily damaged by fighters and by flak, crash-landed upon its return to its Summit base, in Sudan. The Wellesley was a total write-off. Canella would end the campaign with a total of seven confirmed victories to his credit. That morning, he had opened the score of a unit that would be the most successful CR.42 operator by far.

The next day the biplane fighter units were active in their first offensive operations against French airfields in Provence and Tunisia. Strafing Hyères, near the naval base of Toulon, the aircraft of 151° *Gruppo*, with support from 363ª *Squadriglia* of 150° *Gruppo*, claimed to have damaged around '20 aircraft' on the ground. Sergente Maggiore Dino Carta of 366ª *Squadriglia* engaged a Vought 156 of AB3 and shot it down.

On 14 June 412ª *Squadriglia* was back in action in Eritrea when Tenente Mario Visintini shot down Wellesley K7743 of No 14 Sqn over Massawa. A veteran of the Spanish Civil War, where he had claimed at least one aerial victory flying the CR.32, he would subsequently become the leading biplane ace of World War 2 with 16 or 17 individual aerial kills to his credit.

Born in Parenzo on 26 April 1913 into an Italian family at a time when Istria was still part of the Austro-Hungarian Empire, Visintini saw his hometown annexed by Italy when he was just six. From then on he was an Italian citizen. Visintini tried to enlist in the air force immediately after leaving secondary school but was rejected. He persisted and was finally able to enrol in the flying school for non-commissioned officers, obtaining his military wings in September 1937. Two months later he was in Spain, a volunteer with 25ª *Squadriglia*, which was controlled by *XVI Gruppo* of the *Aviazione Legionaria*. Seeing action through to October 1938, Visintini returned home with at least one victory to his name. This success in Spain earned the future ace a permanent air force commission, and he was posted to 4° *Stormo*. This unit was duly transferred to East Africa in April 1940.

In the following months prior to his untimely death in a flying accident, Visintini would become the *Regia Aeronautica's* leading ace. His score was later surpassed by other Italian pilots, but not before 1942. The total loss of all of his unit's documents has meant that Visintini's career has had to be reconstructed from the memories of his *squadriglia* CO and some official papers connected with his decorations or exploits quoted in wartime bulletins.

As detailed in the introduction to this book, CR.42 units flew their last offensive operations against France on 15 June. Exactly one week later France surrendered, and the *Falco* units saw no further action against the *Armée de l'Air*.

In the meantime, combat was escalating over North Africa, where the *Aeronautica della Libia* was confronting the RAF's No 202 Group. On 19 June the machines that would be the protagonists of the early air war over the

This CR.42 proudly wears the 91ª *Squadriglia*, 10° *Gruppo*, 4° *Stormo CT* griffin on its wheel spat in the late summer of 1940. The unit emblem was painted on the aircraft at Goriza prior to the *Squadriglia* heading to North Africa, and it represented the same griffin that had been the unit's insignia in World War 1. During the latter conflict, 91ª *Squadriglia* had been the most successful fighter outfit in the Italian air force. This photograph was probably taken at El Adem or Bengasi Berka – the only two airfields large enough to have a concrete hardstanding like the one seen here (*Renato Zavattini*)

Colonello Arrigo Tessari, CO of 53° *Stormo*, poses with his aircraft on 10 October 1940. Tessari had claimed four shared victories on 15 June during the short French campaign (*Arturo Reiner*)

Mediterranean and Middle East met for the first time. That morning over Sollum, on the border between Egypt and Libya, four No 33 Sqn Gladiators, reinforced by a single Hurricane I of No 80 Sqn flown by future ace Flg Off Peter Wykeham-Barnes, met five CR.42s from 84ª *Squadriglia* of the Tobruk-based 10° *Gruppo*. The Italians, orbiting at 6500 ft while escorting Breda Ba.65 ground attack aircraft, were surprised by the RAF fighters. 84ª *Squadriglia* CO Tenente Colonello Armando Piragino and Sergente Maggiore Ugo Corsi were both lost, and in return a single victory was claimed by Sergente Giuseppe Scaglioni, who recalled;

Giulio Torresi was born in Ancona on 6 February 1915. He gained his wings on 4 November 1935, after which he was posted to 2° *Stormo*. Following service with several reconnaissance units, Torresi became a fighter pilot once again when he joined 1° *Stormo*. Given a permanent commission in the air force in late 1938, he was transferred to 2° *Stormo* in Libya in July 1939. At the beginning of the war Torresi was promoted to tenente, after which he moved to 77ª *Squadriglia*, 13° *Gruppo*. He enjoyed early successes in the CR.42, claiming two Blenheims on 28 June 1940 as his first victories. He then downed Gladiators on 23 and 24 July, followed by a pair of Blenheims that were raiding Gambut on 9 December. After the Italian surrender in September 1943, Torresi served in the *Aeronautica Nazionale Repubblicana*, and he was killed on 1 July 1944 when his Fiat G.55 was shot down by P-47Ds of the 66th FS/57th FG (*Author's collection*)

'As we flew over Bir el Gib we were surprised by a number of Glosters and a Hurricane, which attacked with a height advantage, giving us a lot of trouble. I saw the CO doing a violent manoeuvre while I was breaking to the left. This put me behind a Gloster, which I shot down with my 12.7 mm guns. I immediately lost sight of the CO, and after landing I knew he was missing. In the same combat we lost Sergente Maggiore Corsi, who was shot down by a Hurricane that I vainly attacked in an effort to distract its pilot.'

Scaglioni had downed the Gladiator of Sgt Green, while both the CR.42s lost in this first encounter fell to the Hurricane.

The *Gruppi* of 2° *Stormo* had by then completed their conversion onto the CR.42, and on 28 June they encountered Blenheim IVs from No 113 Sqn that were sent to reconnoitre Tobruk. At least three Blenheim IVs were downed. Although the Italian pilots lost one of their number when Sottotenente Gianmario Zuccarini was forced to crash-land after being hit by defensive fire, they had claimed six victories, and two of them represented the first attributed to Tenente Giulio Torresi.

During the early war years, the *Regia Aeronautica* did not usually attribute victories to individual pilots. Enemy aircraft shot down were generally credited to all the pilots participating in the action. This rule was intended to avoid an individualistic attitude developing amongst fighter pilots, as well as to foster team spirit, but it was not universally observed. Most unit COs followed the rule, although personal claims were normally recorded in combat reports.

One of the units to adopt this practice was 13° *Gruppo*, and this makes it possible to accurately reconstruct Giulio Torresi's victories. Later assigned to 22° *Gruppo*, he went to the Soviet Union, where, between autumn 1941 and spring

Sergente Maggiore Luigi Baron was another early war CR.42 ace, and he is seen here at the controls of his unmarked 412ª *Squadriglia* machine in late 1940. Often flying as wingman to Tenente Visintini, Baron was the second most successful CR.42 ace with 12 and 2 shared victories. All were claimed over East Africa between 30 June 1940 and 25 March 1941, Baron's haul consisting of three Wellesleys, four Blenheims (two shared), one Lysander, four Gladiators and two Hurricanes (*Nicola Malizia*)

1942, he claimed more victories. But *22° Gruppo* was a unit that adhered to the rules, and Torresi was given no individual credits for these successes. Once back home he was to claim his last four victories during the defence of southern Italy and Sicily.

The last day of June 1940 saw 412ª *Squadriglia* claim another Wellesley victory when L2654 of No 223 Sqn failed to return from a raid on Massawa. The CR.42 unit actually claimed two kills, although only one bomber was lost. Sergente Luigi Baron was credited with downing one of them.

By the end of June, the first 20 days of the *Regia Aeronautica's* involvement in World War 2 had seen CR.42 units operating on the three main fronts to which Italian troops had been committed. Pilots flying the biplane fighter had shot down at least 14 enemy aircraft and damaged many more. In return, seven *Falcos* had been downed in combat, with three pilots killed and three others taken prisoner. But this positive balance does not tell the full story. During the same period, flying accidents had accounted for at least eight more Fiats, with the loss of five pilots and the capture of two more. At least two fighters had been burned out on the ground during bombing raids, but worse still was the fact that the units based in North Africa were experiencing severe technical problems with their aircraft. Sand and dust was reducing the useful life of the fighter's Fiat A.74R radial engine to a mere 20-30 hours. It was also causing the aircraft's guns to jam.

The number of CR.42s forced to undergo major overhauls as a result of these problems is not known, but it is likely that as many as 30 machines required urgent maintenance in June alone. In the meantime, the Fiat-Aeritalia factory in Turin had only been able to turn out 40 replacement airframes. The month of July, therefore, started inauspiciously for the CR.42 units.

In North Africa the first skirmishes over the frontline had seen the increasingly aggressive appearance of Gladiator-equipped units. In fact No 33 Sqn, together with a small detachment from No 112 Sqn, patrolling directly over the Italian advanced landing grounds in the area of Capuzzo and Bardia had been able to shoot down a number of CR.32s and Ro.37s in the last days of June. By doing so they had established a certain degree of air superiority over the Italian units in-theatre. The *Aeronautica della Libia* had been unable to deploy the CR.42s of 10° and 13° *Gruppo* to counter the British fighters because their aircraft, having already been worn out in the first 20 days of operations, had been transferred back to the Benghazi area for urgent maintenance. But 8° *Gruppo* had just re-equipped with the new type, and a detachment from its battle-tested 94ª *Squadriglia* was swiftly moved to the airstrip at Menastir, on the Mediterranean coast near the Libyan-Egyptian border.

During the morning of 4 July the unit encountered Gladiators for the first time, and Tenente Giovanni Tadini and Sergente Maggiore Arturo Cardano were both shot down and captured. In an attempt to avenge this defeat, an ill-fated scramble by *Falcos* from 94ª *Squadriglia* against two flights of Gladiators already orbiting over Menastir saw four more CR.42s lost in the late afternoon. Capitano Franco Lavelli and Sergente Maggiores Trento Cecchi and Agostino Fausti all perished, while Sottotenente Nunzio De Fraia parachuted to safety. No 112 Sqn claimed

Sergente Maggiore Agostino Fausti claimed four kills with the CR.42 in just two combats in June-July 1940. Having downed two Blenheims over Tobruk on 29 June whilst serving with 77ª *Squadriglia,* 13° *Gruppo*, he was then temporarily transferred to to 8° *Gruppo*. On the morning of 4 July Fausti claimed two Gladiators, and that afternoon he scrambled to intercept Gladiators of No 33 Sqn. Following the demise of all three of his comrades early on in the engagement, he proceeded to fight the whole British formation single-handedly. He was reported to have damaged two of the enemy fighters, which were forced to leave the combat area just before Fausti was shot down and killed. During this last combat it is probable that he had shot down Gladiator N5751 of Flg Off Price-Owen, thus taking his tally to five. This victory remained unconfirmed, however. Fausti was awarded a posthumous *Medaglia d'oro al valor militare* – he was the first *Falco* pilot to receive Italy's highest wartime decoration (*Italian Air Force*)

Maggiore Ernesto Botto, CO of 9° *Gruppo*, is seen at Comiso during the summer of 1940. A living legend in the Italian armed forces, Botto volunteered to serve in Spain during the spring of 1937 and took command of 32ª *Squadra VI Gruppo* of *Aviazione Legionaria*. During the summer and autumn of 1937, he claimed four individual victories and several shared kills. However, on 12 October 1937 the CR.32s of his *gruppo* were surprised by Republican I-15s and I-16s over Fuentes de l'Ebro and they suffered a serious defeat. Five were shot down, with three pilots captured and two killed, in exchange for two I-16s and a I-15 shot down and a Russian pilot killed. Botto claimed his fifth victory (an I-16) during the clash, but he also suffered a serious wound to his right thigh. He somehow managed to limp back to base, but his leg had to be amputated. For his conduct, Botto received the *Medaglia d'oro al valor militare*, thus becoming one of the few recipients to be awarded this decoration whilst still alive. Back in Italy, he refused to accept that he could no longer fly, learning to do so with an artificial leg. He regained his wings and the command of 73ª *Squadriglia* of 9° *Gruppo* in 1938, and on 1 November 1939 Botto took command of 9° *Gruppo* itself Meanwhile, a triangular badge depicting 'an iron leg' had appeared on the tail fins of the unit's Fiat fighters, and this continued as an unofficial *gruppo* insignia until the spring of 1942. *'Gamba di ferro'* ('iron leg') was Botto's nickname (*Fulvio Chianese – Associazione Culturale 4° Stormo di Gorizia*)

nine victories during the course of the day, with Flg Off Tony Worcester being credited with four of them.

This aggressive patrolling over Italian bases also brought success for the RAF squadrons operating in another sector. On 2 July, over the Eritrean township of Assab, three Gladiators from Aden-based No 94 Sqn had surprised two *Falcos* of the resident 414ª *Squadriglia* as they took off. Both Italian fighters were quickly shot down. The annihilation of the *squadriglia* was completed on the 10th with the destruction of its last fighters on the ground by three Gladiators and a Blenheim from No 8 Sqn. The unit, having lost all six of its CR.42s, was disbanded and no more aircraft were based on the exposed airfield of Assab.

These combats had demonstrated that not only was the more manoeuvrable Gladiator a deadly opponent for the *Falco*, but that if surprised at low altitude or during take-off by the aggressive RAF pilots, the Italian biplane fighter had little chance of escaping unscathed. Despite these reversals, some CR.42 pilots were still achieving success, as Visintini clearly demonstrated when he shot down another Wellesley from No 14 Sqn on 3 July.

The first week of July 1940 had also seen the CR.42 make its combat debut on yet another front when 9° *Gruppo* received orders to move to the Sicilian airfield of Comiso for operations over Malta. The *gruppo* was then based at Turin-Mirafiori. The *Regia Aeronautica* believed that the CR.42 would be a better match for the handful of Sea Gladiators then defending the island than the C.200s of 6° *Gruppo Autonomo*, which were already in Sicily. On 3 July, two days after their arrival, a dozen 9° *Gruppo* pilot took off as escorts for a pair of SM.79 bombers that had been sent to reconnoitre Malta. The *gruppo* diary reported;

'The conduct of the two SM.79s was quite unpredictable, and all the island defences were alerted. When one of them closed on the target it was suddenly attacked by two enemy fighters of the "Spitfire" type. One of the two fighters was immediately attacked by Maggiore Ernesto Botto, who kept firing for some time until he finally saw it go down.'

Botto had shot down Hurricane I P2614 of the Malta Fighter Flight, piloted by Flg Off John Waters. The fighter had to be written off after it crash-landed, the Hurricane's loss avenging the destruction of one of the Savoia-Marchetti bombers that Waters had managed to shoot down prior to his own demise.

A few days later 9° *Gruppo* was ordered to Libya to help make good the losses being suffered by the units based there. Its place in the battle for Malta was taken by 23° *Gruppo*, now detached from 3° *Stormo* and operating autonomously. The *gruppo's* CR.42s, flying mainly visual reconnaissance and escort missions, frequently encountered aircraft from the local Fighter Flight, which was soon to become No 261 Sqn. The Italian pilots were able to claim significant successes, with Hurricane I P2653 (flown by Plt Off W R C 'Dick' Sugden) heavily damaged on the 13 July, Flt Lt Peter Keeble shot down in Hurricane I P2623 on the 16th, and a Swordfish floatplane destroyed on the 21st, the latter being jointly shared with a CR.42 pilot from 17° *Gruppo*.

The last day of July saw CR.42s and Sea Gladiators clash for the first, and only, time over Malta. The engagement ended with one loss on either side, future ace Flg Off W J Woods shooting down the machine of Capitano Antonio Chiodi, who lost his life, while Capitano Luigi Filippi (also a future ace), recently returned from France after having been captured on 15 June, shot down N5519 piloted by Flg Off Peter Hartley. Apart from Chiodi, the only other Italian loss of the month had been Sottotenente Mario Benedetti, who had died on the 16th in the same action that that had seen Tenenti Mario Pinna and Oscar Abello jointly down Keeble.

Maggiore Ernesto Botto, CO of 9° *Gruppo*, returns from a mission in CR.42 MM4393. To make him more easily recognisable to his pilots in combat – all *Falcos* lacked radios – he wore a red leather flying helmet. Having scored five victories during the Spanish Civil War while flying the CR.32, Botto went on to claim three more kills during World War 2 in the CR.42. The first of these came on 3 July 1940 when he claimed to have shot down a Hurricane over Malta. 9° *Gruppo* then moved to North Africa, where Botto was credited with destroying a Blenheim on 12 October and a Hurricane on 9 December 1940 (*Author's collection*)

In North Africa, the serviceability crisis of June and early July, which was caused mainly through the lack of sand filters in-theatre for the CR.42s, was being overcome. Units slowly started to reappear over the frontline in strength, although the recent beating suffered by 8° *Gruppo* rendered all *Falco* pilots much more cautious towards the Gladiators. In a series of combats during three consecutive days towards the end of July, as many as four Gladiators from Nos 33 and 112 Sqns were claimed destroyed by CR.42 pilots for the loss of just one machine in return.

During the first of these combats, in the late afternoon of 23 July, future *Falco* ace Tenente Guglielmo Chiarini claimed his first victory of the war when he shot down Plt Off Preston of No 33 Sqn in N5774. Chiarini was part of a nine-strong 13° *Gruppo* formation that had intercepted three Gladiators flying in a broad 'vic' as escorts for a Lysander on a reconnaissance mission. He had succeeded in downing Preston after a ten-minute dogfight, the latter bailing out south of Bardia.

The following day Tenente Enzo Martissa of 91ª *Squadriglia* forced Sgt Shaw of No 33 Sqn to make a crash-landing. During a subsequent patrol over the frontline he returned to finish the fighter off. On the morning of the 25th three of Tenente Chiarini's comrades from 77ª and 78ª *Squadriglie* turned the tables on a mixed formation of Gladiators from Nos 112 and 33 Sqns that had bounced them over Bardia. Although outnumbered by their opponents, Sergente Maggiore Leone Basso and Sergente Rovero Abbarchi claimed the destruction of Flg Off Strahan's Gladiator after a spirited battle. Sgt Slater was also seen to spin down out of the fight and force-land. Canadian ace Plt Off V C 'Woody' Woodward, who claimed two CR.42s destroyed following this clash,

An impressive line up of CR.42s from 18° *Gruppo* at Mirafori in August 1940. The aircraft with the white band just forward of its tailpane was the personal machine of *Gruppo* CO, Maggiore Ferruccio Vosilla (*Giuseppe Ruzzin via Giandrea Bussi*)

High-scoring ace Franco Lucchini of 90ª *Squadriglia*, 10° *Gruppo*, was born in Rome on 24 December 1914. He too fought in Spain in 1937-38, where he was credited with a number of victories prior to being shot down and captured. Once back in Italy after the war, Lucchini received a permanent commission in the air force and was posted to 4° *Stormo*. Assigned to 90ª *Squadriglia*, he claimed a number of shared victories (between 5 and 15) flying CR.42s in North Africa before returning to Italy. Post-war studies have shown that three of these victories actually represented individual kills over a Sunderland (L2160/X of No 230 Sqn, piloted by Wg Cdr G Francis, which was only badly damaged) on 21 June 1940, a Gladiator (K7910 of No 80 Sqn, piloted by the RAF's future 'ace of aces' Flt Lt 'Pat' Pattle) on 4 August 1940 and a Hurricane (of No 274 Sqn, flown by Plt Off McFadden who was detached from No 73 Sqn) on 16 December 1940. Lucchini later raised his score to 22 individual and 52 shared victories. At the time of his death in combat in a C.202 on 5 July 1943, Lucchini was the *Regia Aeronautica's* top-scoring pilot. He received a posthumous *Medaglia d'oro al valor militare* (*via Ali di Guerra*)

recalled, 'They were clean fighters those "Wops", and quite the equal of any Hun when it came to combat flying'.

The final CR.42 victory of July came on the 29th when Libya-based *Falcos* shot down Blenheim IF K7178 of No 30 Sqn and heavily damaged a Blenheim IV of No 113 Sqn. However, Sergente Scaglioni, who had shared these victories with Tenente Franco Lucchini of 90ª *Squadriglia*, crashed on landing after his CR.42 had been damaged by return fire.

Results for the *Falco* units in East Africa also improved in the second half of July following the disastrous start to the month at Assab. 413ª *Squadriglia* downed Gladiator L9042, flown by Plt Off Carter of No 94 Sqn on the 13th, while 412ª *Squadriglia* destroyed five more Wellesleys on the 12th, 16th (two), 23rd and the 29th.

By month-end, at least 16 victories had been credited to CR.42 pilots operating on a handful of fronts for the loss of ten *Falcos* in combat. Aircraft destroyed on the ground due to other causes had again been high, however. But the mechanical problems caused by sand were being remedied through the installation of sand filters for the engines' carburettor air intakes. Additional oil coolers were also being installed and special canvas sand covers for guns, propellers, engines and landing gear were now being used too. This would finally end the continuous mechanical wastage that had characterised the first two months of CR.42 operations over North Africa in particular.

August opened with an increase in the intensity of air operations as 4° *Stormo*, now with both its *Gruppi* – 9° and 10° – fully operational over North Africa, struggled to gain aerial superiority. Formations of 30 CR.42s stepped at different heights now started to appear over the front, and on 4 August one such group intercepted Blenheim Is from No 211 Sqn. At least one machine (L8532) was brought down. While returning to base, the *Falco* pilots engaged lone Gladiator K7910, flown by future ranking RAF ace Flt Lt 'Pat' Pattle of No 80 Sqn. The latter had just claimed his first victory during a wild low-level dogfight with Ba.65s and escorting CR.32s. Attacking the isolated fighter from all angles, the Italian pilots were able to claim its destruction, which, in a rare case of individual credit, was attributed to ace Tenente Franco Lucchini.

Two days later, Capitano Luigi Monti of 84ª *Squadriglia* was able to down Sunderland N9025 of No 228 Sqn off Bardia, the flying-boat having been shadowing an Italian convoy in the Mediterranean. This was the first example of its type to fall to the guns of an Italian fighter in-theatre. Back over the frontline, 4° *Stormo's* efforts to establish air superiority for the Italians seemed nearly complete by the end of the first week of August. However, on the 8th No 80 Sqn executed a perfect ambush, exploiting the superiority of its Gladiators over the Italian biplanes to maximum effect.

Led by Sqn Ldr P H 'Paddy' Dunn, who handed over tactical control of the action to Pattle, no fewer than 13 Gladiators were able to position themselves in the classic 'six o'clock high' position above 16 *Falcos* from 9° and 10° *Gruppi*. Led by Maggiore Carlo Romagnoli, the latter were slowly climbing out from their base at El Adem, heading for their initial patrol point. As the CR.42s passed over Bir El Gobi – still well inside Italian territory – the Gladiators attacked from above. After a devastating first pass, the RAF pilots engaged their foes in a low-level dogfight. Radio

CR.42 MM4308 was being flown by Tenente Enzo Martissa of 91ª *Squadriglia* on 8 August 1940 when he was shot down by Gladiators of No 80 Sqn. Martissa, who was initially posted missing, had force-landed his CR.42, riddled with more than 100 bullet holes, only nine miles from El Adem. The badly wounded pilot claimed the individual destruction of two Gladiators, which were credited to him in post-war studies. Unable to leave his *Falco* due to his injuries, Martissa survived his ordeal by drinking the dew at dawn. After two days he was beginning to expect the worst. One of the bullets that had hit his aircraft had pierced the *squadriglia's* griffin's head badge (see page 13) on the port wheel spat. With a knife, Martissa scratched on the white background to the insignia, 'You, little griffin, have been struck in the head. I would have suffered less if I had also been! I'm not mortally wounded, but I shall die, for I can't walk for 10-20 km to reach a track. And it will be my hunger and thirst that gets me'. Fortunately for Martissa, patrolling Italian troops found him on 10 August. A very promising pilot who was a veteran of the Spanish Civil War, he had already claimed a Blenheim destroyed and a share in one as a probable prior to downing the Gladiators. Once back in Italy, Martissa was not to see further active service, however. MM4308 was recovered and repaired, and in September 1940 it was assigned to 84ª *Squadriglia* of 10° *Gruppo* as '84-4' (*Fulvio Chianese – Associazione Culturale 4° Stormo di Gorizia*)

control had been a critical factor in gaining the initial surprise, and the Gladiator's superior horizontal manoeuvrability helped finish the job.

By the time the clash had ended, eight Italian fighters had been destroyed. 73ª *Squadriglia* had been hit the hardest, losing five aircraft in the first pass. Sergentes Enrico Dallari and Antonio Valle bailed out, Sottotenente Alvaro Querci and Sergente Santo Gino force-landed and Maresciallo Norino Renzi was killed. Sergente Lido Poli was also hit early in the fight, being severely wounded in the left arm. Despite this injury, he continued to fight, claiming to have shot down one Gladiator before force-landing close to an infantry unit. Poli was sent back to El Adem, where his arm had to be amputated. For his courageous display he was awarded the *Medaglia d'oro al valor militare*, Poli becoming the first non-posthumous recipient of Italy's highest military decoration in World War 2. Sergente Aldo Rosa was slightly wounded and bailed out, while Tenente Enzo Martissa force-landed with wounds.

Despite being badly disorganised, and having been taken completely by surprise, the surviving CR.42 pilots had stubbornly remained in the fight, shooting down the machines of Flt Sgt Vaughan (K7903), who was killed, and Flt Lt Evers-Swindell (L8010). Flg Off Flower's K8011 suffered a damaged engine, and he was forced to leave the fray. This air battle represented a serious setback for 4° *Stormo*, with the unit suffering its worst combat losses on a single day for the entire war. Once again the *Regia Aeronautica* became more cautious in its approach to tackling the

Two pilots of 95ª *Squadriglia,* 18° *Gruppo* enjoy a lighter moment as they jokingly kiss the ground to celebrate their safe crossing of the Mediterranean from Pantelleria to Zuara, in Cyrenaica, in mid-August 1940. The CR.42 pictured is MM4332. At this time the *Gruppo* was fully occupied ferrying *Falcos* to Castelbenito (*Giorgio Apostolo*)

CR.42 '85-9', flown by Tenente Giulio Cesare Giuntella of 85ª *Squadriglia,* 18° *Gruppo,* cruises past over Mount Etna on 10 August 1940. Giuntella made shared claims for three French fighters shot down during the Italian attacks on airfields in Provence in June 1940. Later, he took part in the *CAI* operations over England, and subsequently served as CO of 85ª *Squadriglia* (*Giuseppe Ruzzin via Giandrea Bussi*)

RAF, and this action virtually ended the month's fighter action on the Libyan front. No 80 Sqn had also suffered losses, however, with six Gladiators destroyed, two pilots killed and one wounded in its first week of operations. Such a rate of loss was not sustainable.

In East Africa, Italian troops launched an offensive to subdue British Somaliland in early August. They were covered by the CR.42s of 413ª *Squadriglia* and the CR.32s of 410ª *Squadriglia.* On the 8th, as part of the campaign, the *Regia Aeronautica* retaliated against the Assab attacks of the previous month with a raid on the airstrip at Berbera. Two CR.32s and a solitary CR.42 strafed two No 94 Sqn Gladiators that had been detached here to help stiffen the base's defences.

Wearing a bulky life-vest over his flying overall, Maresciallo Giuseppe Ruzzin of 85ª *Squadriglia,* 18° *Gruppo* poses in front of his CR.42 at Pantelleria on 11 August 1940. The *Gruppo* was busy ferrying 30 CR.42s to Castel Benito, in Cyrenaica, when this photograph was taken. By the time Ruzzin left 18° *Gruppo* he had flown a total of 150 hours in the CR.42, of which 72 were in combat. He thought that the *Falco* was a great aircraft to fly, just as its predecessor the CR.32 had been. It was, however, slightly nose-heavy, and inclined to lose height during aerobatics. One big advantage it had over the CR.32 (and the Gladiator, for that matter) was it variable-pitch propeller (*Giuseppe Ruzzin via Giandrea Bussi*)

Subsequent operations over British Somaliland resulted in many engagements between the CR.42s of 413ª *Squadriglia* and the Aden-based Blenheim Is of No 39 Sqn, which lost its first machine (L8387) to the Italian fighters on 12 August. To the north, 412ª *Squadriglia* was also enjoying continued success against RAF Wellesleys, with an aircraft from No 14 Sqn being forced down on the 4th and one from No 47 Sqn suffering a similar same fate five days later.

NIGHTFIGHTER

The night of 13/14 August was to see a very special CR.42 exploit on yet another front. Since Italy had declared war on Britain and France, RAF Bomber Command had been undertaking a series of raids against targets in the industrial north of the country. That night, the CR.42s of 150° *Gruppo* made a series of scrambles against bombers detected over Turin. At 0155 hrs, ten minutes after take-off, Capitano Giorgio Graffer, CO of 365ª *Squadriglia,* engaged a British bomber flying over the Fiat factory. He reported;

Capitano Corrado Santoro claimed four victories while flying the CR.42. His first success was a Blenheim downed on 20 August 1940 over Diredawa, in East Africa, while serving with 413ª *Squadriglia*. Joining 370ª *Squadriglia* in 1941, he claimed three 'Hurricanes' destroyed and three more as probables on 27 September 1941 in an action fought 125 miles off Sardinia. His victims were, in fact, fighters from HMS *Ark Royal,* which lost two 808 NAS Fulmars reportedly to 'friendly' AA fire from escorting naval vessels. These victories were only claimed by Santoro in his logbook, not officially. According to other sources, Santoro stated that he had downed two 'Hurricanes'. He stayed in the air force post-war and retired with the rank of generale di divisione (*Sergio Santoro*)

'On the night of 14 August I was ordered to scramble over Turin. I took off with a wingman to intercept enemy aircraft reported by the flak defence. Each of us started to search independently, and I was lucky enough to spot an enemy aircraft by the flames coming from its exhausts. I attacked from astern and it returned fire, hitting my engine. I tried to shoot at it from below but my guns refused to fire and my engine was losing oil. Considering that my aeroplane was close to the end of its life, I decided to try and ram the enemy machine and escape by parachute.

'I flew over the enemy but the airflow from its airscrews caused my aeroplane to become inverted, so my first attempt failed. I flew alongside the enemy aircraft and hit its tailplane with my airscrew. My aeroplane spun down and I abandoned it. I acted in this way because I believed that my aircraft had been allocated to me for use against the enemy in any way I saw fit. My action, although quite dangerous, was not suicidal.'

Hit in one engine, and with its starboard aileron severely damaged by the fire from Graffer's CR.42, Whitley V P4965 of No 10 Sqn now faced the long flight back to its base at Abingdon. Plt Off Parson succeeded in coaxing the crippled bomber across France, but while trying to land at an airfield on the Kent coast, the weakened aileron broke off and the Whitley plunged into the sea. Three of the crew managed to escape, but the two pilots died. Having done his best to down the bomber, Graffer had scrambled out of his crippled fighter wearing only a pair of tennis shorts! The tale of the pilot who had bailed out 'with only his pants on' soon became celebrated in press reports. More significantly, Graffer's exploit represented the first successful night interception by an Italian fighter. The pilot, whose claim had initially been treated with some scepticism, became a celebrity, albeit only for a short period.

Born in Trento on 24 May 1912, Graffer was to become one of Italy's most famous mountaineers. He had joined the *Regia Aeronautica* as a permanent officer in 1931, and during the Spanish Civil War period he served with 2° *Stormo* in Libya, thus ruling him out of participation in the conflict. An extremely competent and aggressive pilot, Graffer had led the strafing section of 150° *Gruppo* over Cuers Pierrefeu on 15 June 1940, sharing in the aerial victories claimed that day.

On 15 August it was again the turn of the units based in Sicily to achieve success when Tenente Leopoldo Sartirana of 17° *Gruppo* claimed

The CR.42 of Capitano Corrado Santoro of 413ª *Squadriglia* displays signs of battle damage. Shortly after dawn on 20 August 1940, four No 39 Sqn Blenheims and one from No 11 Sqn attacked the Ala Littoria hangar at Diredawa, in East Africa. Their bombs started a fire that damaged an S.81 under repair in the hangar, and shrapnel also holed a CR.32. Approaching the target, the bombers had been attacked by two CR.42s of 413ª *Squadriglia,* and Plt Off P E O Jago's Blenheim was shot down in flames by Santoro. He also hit the sole No 11 Sqn aircraft, which crash-landed upon its return to Aden. Santoro's aircraft was damaged by return fire, however (*Sergio Santoro*)

to have shot down Hurricane N2716 of No 261 Sqn, piloted by Sgt Roy O'Donnell, whilst escorting SM.79s.

Five days later, over Diredawa, in central Ethiopia, Capitano Corrado Santoro scored a double victory. Intercepting a raid by five Aden-based Blenheim Is, he was able to shoot down L8474 of No 39 Sqn and damage another from No 11 Sqn, which later crash-landed at its base.

On 24 August 17 CR.42s of 23° *Gruppo*, escorting six SM.79s over Malta, thwarted an attack by four Hurricanes. Tenente Mario Rigatti was able to damage the aircraft of Flt Lt George Burges, who crash-landed N2730 upon his return to base. However, Sergente Maggiore Renzo Bocconi was shot down by Flg Off Taylor and taken prisoner.

Tenente Mario Rigatti of 75ª *Squadriglia* claimed to have shot down a Hurricane over Malta while flying CR.42 MM4382 '75-6' on 24 August 1940. The aircraft in question was probably N2730, flown by future ace Flt Lt George Burges of No 261 Sqn. Moments later Rigatti was seriously wounded in the leg by the fire from another Hurricane, possibly flown by Plt Off Thomas Balmforth. Barely able to fly his damaged aircraft back to base, Rigatti had to have his leg amputated. In a story reminiscent of Ernesto Botto's, Rigatti would learn how to fly with an artificial leg and rejoin his unit at the end of 1942. He too would receive the *Medaglia d'oro al valor militare*. The Malta Hurricane was the only individual victory credited to Rigatti in the CR.42 (*Nicola Malizia*)

The month closed for 412ª *Squadriglia* with more success on the 26th when the unit downed Wellesley K7731 of No 223 Sqn. By the end of August CR.42 pilots had claimed at least 14 victories for the loss of 11 *Falcos* in combat – almost all of them sustained in the disastrous dogfight of the 8th. However, with fewer losses to non-operational causes, the CR.42-equipped fighter units were gradually starting to build up their strength.

AUTUMN LULL

September opened with another success for 412ª *Squadriglia* on the 1st when Tenente Visintini scrambled from Massawa and shot down Wellesley L2689 of No 14 Sqn. Later, the episode was woven into a propaganda tale by the Italians in which the Wellesley, transformed into a Blenheim, had been deliberately captured intact by the Italian ace. He had reputedly organised an ambush of the aircraft with the aim of studying its flying characteristics. Whether the story is real or not, the damaged machine had been forced to crash-land on Harmil Island, inside Italian territory, where the crew was captured.

CR.42s from 92ª *Squadriglia*, 8° *Gruppo* are seen at a typical desert airfield in Libya in the autumn of 1940. The aircraft are probably on standby duty since their engines have no coverings – essential in the dusty conditions of North Africa. Note also the bottles of compressed air placed nearby to start the engines when the call comes. Engines were usually started using a single-cylinder pull-start two-stroke Garelli motor. This was fitted into the aircraft to the right and behind the pilot, its job being to build up enough compressed air to tick over the main engine (*Giorgio Apostolo*)

Sergente Maggiore Davide Colauzzi (left), Capitano Bruno Locatelli (CO) and possibly Sottotenente Furio Lauri of 368ª *Squadriglia*, 151° *Gruppo* pose for a photograph at Pantelleria during the move to North Africa on 8 September 1940. All three men claimed victories while flying the CR.42. Locatelli, from Como, was a permanent officer who had served as an instructor with the the *Accademia Aeronautica* during the Spanish Civil War. Rejoining 368ª *Squadriglia* in 1938, he participated in the first strafing attack of the war on 13 June. Locatelli kept meticulous records of his unit's achievements, and these are among the more reliable to be found in the archives of the *Regia Aeronautica*. Despite being an aggressive and skilled pilot, Locatelli only claimed shared victories in accordance with official air force policy. Shot down by AA fire at the end of January 1941, he ended the war in Yol PoW camp. By then he had claimed shares in at least two Hurricanes and three Blenheims that his unit had downed, as well as two probable victories (*Enrico Locatelli*)

CR.42s of 368ª *Squadriglia*, 151° *Gruppo* escort a bomber over the Mediterranean in late 1940. This *gruppo* was the first to receive the CR.42, in March 1939, and it moved to North Africa in September 1940. The unit remained in Libya until 31 July 1941, when it was withdrawn to Treviso for a rest. At the end of November 151° *Gruppo* returned to North Africa, and it continued to fly CR.42s in-theatre until 30 December, when its surviving *Falcos* were sent to 60° *Gruppo* (*Giorgio Apostolo*)

The following day, Sergente Ernesto Pavan of 92ª *Squadriglia*, 8° *Gruppo*, scrambled from Derna, where he was on standby duty, and intercepted a nuisance raid by two Blenheim Is of No 211 Sqn. Both were shot down. Unit CO Sqn Ldr Bax crash-landed L8376 in Italian territory and was captured, along with his crew. L8471 force-landed at Sidi el-Barrani and was recovered.

On 4 September action flared on another front when 13 Swordfish from the aircraft carrier HMS *Eagle* attempted to raid Maritza airfield on the island of Rhodes. The defences, alerted by a previous attack, were able to scramble a mixed group of CR.32s and CR.42s from the resident 163ª *Squadriglia Autonoma*. Although two Fiats collided during the hurried take-off, the others were able to repel the attack, downing four of the bombers for the loss of a single CR.32. Twelve British airmen failed to return, eight of them being taken prisoner, and two Swordfish were captured intact.

Four days later, over central Ethiopia, a CR.42 of 413ª *Squadriglia* shot down a Martin Maryland I of No 8 Sqn, killing all bar one member of the crew. This was followed up on 10 September by the destruction of yet another Wellesley of No 14 Sqn, which crashed neat Kassala after being attacked by a *Falco* from 412ª *Squadriglia*.

On 13 September Marshal Rodolfo Graziani's army launched an offensive in North Africa with the aim of capturing Sidi el Barrani, in Egypt, from the British. In an effort to strengthen the fighter force in-theatre prior to the commencement of this campaign, the *Regia Aeronautica* despatched a fifth fighter group in the form of 151° *Gruppo*, which was now detached from 53° *Stormo* and operating autonomously, from northern Italy to Libya with a full complement of 30 CR.42s.

The RAF fighter units, most of which had been withdrawn to their permanent bases in eastern Egypt in order to make good recent losses, failed to appear over the front during this period. The Blenheims of No 202 Group, however, made a series of raids against Italian troops and rear bases with the aim of slowing their advance down.

On the 18th, just such a raid on Tmimi airfield was tardily intercepted by a section of three CR.42s from 82ª *Squadriglia, 13° Gruppo*, after the nine Blenheim IVs of No 113 Sqn had released their bombs over the Italian airstrip – at least four SM.79s were severely damaged. Tenente Chiarini, who was leading the biplane fighters, shot down the lead Blenheim (T2048), and with the help of his wingmen chased the other bombers until their return fire wounded him. Two more bombers were damaged.

Twenty-four hours earlier on 17 September, 23° *Gruppo* had flown yet another escort mission to Malta (this time protecting Italian Ju 87s). During the course of the operation its pilots had claimed some victories that could not be corroborated by British sources. In return, the CR.42 of Sottotenente Francesco Cavalli had been lost, the aircraft almost certainly falling victim to Flg Off 'Timber' Woods of No 261 Sqn, even if the captured pilot reported that he had been forced to take to his parachute due to his fighter suffering a lubrication system failure that caused his engine to seize. Cavalli's demise took Woods' tally to five victories, thus making him an ace.

An unknown pilot poses on the cockpit coaming of the CR.42 assigned to Maggiore Tito Falconi, CO of 23° *Gruppo Autonomo*. The aircraft is marked up as 70ª *Squadriglia* machine, and it displays a diagonal white band on the fuselage to aid identification in the air. Falconi claimed one victory with the CR.42 on 7 September 1940 when he reported shooting down a No 261 Sqn Hurricane over Valetta (*Nicola Malizia*)

Over North Africa, September ended with a series of encounters between *Falcos* and Blenheims. A No 211 Sqn machine crash-landed on the 25th, another, from No 55 Sqn, was shot down on the 27th by a patrol from 97ª *Squadriglia*, which also severely damaged a second machine of the same unit. Finally, a No 113 Sqn bomber was lost with its crew to a trio of fighters from 13° *Gruppo* on the 30th. That same day also saw the Blenheim I make its first appearance over the northern front in East Africa when elements of No 45 Sqn, temporarily detached from Egypt, started operations there. During a raid on Gura – 412ª *Squadriglia's* nest – L6665 of Flt Lt G J Bush was shot down with the loss of its crew. This aircraft was possibly another victim of Tenente Visintini, who was credited with shooting down two Blenheims over Gura during this period.

Falco units had reported destroying at least 15 bombers for just a single loss in combat during September. And despite the Fiat factory being unable to increase its output beyond the usual 40 machines that month, the CR.42 *squadriglie* continued to build up their strength. October brought an increase in the intensity of air operations as *'Il Duce'*, Benito Mussolini, in an attempt to shift the balance of power within the Axis alliance more in his favour, decided to open up two additional war fronts.

CR.42s of 85ª *Squadriglia*, 18° *Gruppo* patrol over Genoa harbour during the autumn of 1940. Aircraft '85-2' is being flown by future 19-kill ace Sergente Luigi Gorrini (*Giuseppe Ruzzin via Giandrea Bussi*)

NEW FRONTS OPEN UP

With France's surrender on 22 June 1940 bringing an end to operations for the CR.42-equipped *gruppi* of I^a^ *Squadra Aerea*, the units sat idle for several months at their bases in northwestern Italy. Following the French capitulation, Mussolini began to consider the possibility of sending I^a^ *Squadra Aerea* to Belgium to fight alongside the Luftwaffe as the Battle of Britain reached its climax.

'Il Duce's' plan proceeded despite the opposition of central Air Force HQ in Rome, Generale Corso Fougier being sent to Germany in August to study the situation on the Channel Front. He returned fully aware that the autumn weather conditions that were to be expected by the time the I^a^ *Squadra Aerea* arrived in Belgium were the kind which in the Mediterranean normally kept Italian aircraft firmly grounded. Fougier also understood that the traditional dogfight had been replaced as the premier fighter combat tactic by 'dive' and 'zoom', with great emphasis placed on firepower. Yet the Luftwaffe had clearly shown him, with the aid of data and statistics, that they were close to gaining complete air superiority, and that the resulting situation was one in which the inferior Italian units could be used profitably. Accordingly, the decision to proceed was made in the hope of a quick end to operations.

The *Corpo Aereo Italiano* (*CAI* – Italian Air Corps) was officially formed on 10 September. It included a new fighter *stormo*, 56°, which consisted of 18° *Gruppo* and its CR.42s and 20° *Gruppo* with Fiat G.50s. These units were given the best possible aircraft, with the two *gruppi* receiving factory-fresh machines fitted with the most modern equipment then available to Italian units. For the first time a complete *gruppo* of CR.42s was given the benefit of radios in most of its aircraft, even if they were only the unreliable ARC.1 receivers that were often removed in the frontline in order to save weight. The aircraft also had an additional fuel tank, albeit not self-sealing, but the armament was, in accordance with contemporary practice, reduced to a single Breda-SAFAT 12.7 mm machine gun, with the other weapon replaced by a 7.7 mm weapon.

The *Falcos*, led by Maggiore Ferruccio Vosilla, left Turin-Mirafiori on 16 October and reached Ursel, in Belgium, on the 19th. Once at their new base, the pilots of 18° *Gruppo* started to make contact with their counterparts from the Luftwaffe. The German pilots were highly optimistic about the general trend of the war, despite the severe losses that they had suffered during the Battle of Britain. When the moment came to evaluate the Italian equipment, they frankly expressed the opinion that the CR.42 was not suitable for the conflict. In particular, they were amazed at the total lack of armour protection for the pilots. They also explained the great importance of radio, not only to help with navigation but also for tactical purposes.

At Ursel steps were hastily taken to try to improve the situation. Armour was added to seat backs and the auxiliary fuel tanks were removed, although this meant the short-range Fiats were now only able to reach the eastern parts of Kent or the southeastern areas of Sussex, with an endurance of just ten minutes over the target area. Furthermore, a new type of radio set was tested to replace the useless ARC.1. It offered no improvement, however, and the Italian pilots realised that their only method of communication in action would be by signals such as waggling their wings, shooting off a few rounds or waving their arms, just as they had been doing since World War 1!

Pilots from 18° *Gruppo* are seen in front of their CR.42s at Ursel in October 1940. At left without his life jacket is Capitano Gino Lodi, CO of 95ª *Squadriglia*. Capitano Edoardo Molinari, CO of 83ª *Squadriglia*, is to Lodi's left (*Giorgio Apostolo*)

In the warmer climes of East Africa, where the opposition was more easily dealt with by the *Falco*, the arrival of No 45 Sqn in Sudan in late September had meant an increase in air raids on Eritrea. But the unit had discovered that its primary target – the airfield at Gura – was well defended. Therefore, on top of the losses already suffered on 30 September, a Blenheim was downed on 2 October, followed by two more machines on the 13th. These aircraft fell to 412ª *Squadriglia*, with future ace Sergente Maggiore Luigi Baron claiming both Blenheims on the 2nd.

On the 4th, in the same general area, the Gladiators of the newly equipped No 1 Sqn South African Air Force (SAAF) had met the CR.42s of 412ª *Squadriglia* for the first time over Metemma. Its pilots claimed to have shot down one Fiat for no loss. The Italian pilots apparently claimed a victory in return, although in reality they had only damaged the machine of Capt B J L Boyle. The latter had downed the *Falco* credited to No 1 Sqn, this being the first of five and one shared CR.42s that he would claim destroyed between October 1940 and February 1941.

Although there was plenty of aerial action in East Africa, in North Africa, by contrast, things had been fairly quiet since the capture of Sidi el-Barrani and the halting of the Italian offensive in the latter half of September. Blenheims performed the occasional raid and the Lysanders of No 208 Sqn reconnoitred the frontline in preparation for the Allied counter-offensive. Such operations meant action at last for the CR.42s on 12 October when a trio of No 55 Sqn Blenheim Is made a dusk attack on the main fighter base at El Adem. Scrambling with his CO, Tenente Giulio Reiner of 73ª *Squadriglia*, 9° *Gruppo* was able to claim the destruction of two bombers. Maggiore Botto accounted for the third, although only two RAF aircraft had actually been shot down.

On the 15th, No 208 Sqn Lysander L4714, flown by Plt Off D B M Druce, was intercepted over the front by three fighters from 92ª *Squadriglia*, 8° *Gruppo* led by Tenente Ranieri Piccolomini. The RAF aircraft was quickly shot down, with the loss of the crew.

The next day in East Africa, nine aircraft from 412ª *Squadriglia* carried out an early morning strafing attack on the airstrip at Gedaref, which

Tenente Giulio Reiner stands in front of two 73ª *Squadriglia* CR.42s in North Africa in 1940. He achieved his first victories with the *Falco* on 12 October 1940 when, in combat with three No 55 Sqn Blenheim Is, he claimed two of them destroyed. In fact, one belly-landed and a second was declared damaged beyond repair when it returned to base. Reiner's third kill was claimed while flying a C.202 on 19 August 1942. His fourth victory, however, came in a CR.42. He ended the war with a total of 10 and 57 shared victories, 3 and 1 of which were claimed while flying the CR.42 (*Reiner via Gabriele Brancaccio*)

The brand new CR.42s of 18° *Gruppo* provide the backdrop for this view of *Falco* pilots being briefed by their *Gruppo* CO, Maggiore Ferruccio Vosilla, at Turin-Mirafiori prior to departing for Belgium in October 1940. The aircraft nearest to the camera, marked with a broad white command band around the rear fuselage and rank pennant beneath the cockpit, was assigned to Vosilla himself (*Giorgio Apostolo*)

had recently been occupied by a detachment of eight Wellesleys from No 47 Sqn. Led in by an SM.79, the fighters were under the command of unit CO, Capitano Raffi. The Fiat pilots, including Tenente Visintini, claimed the destruction of 11 enemy aircraft on the ground, together with a munitions dump and a truck. In fact, they had destroyed all eight Wellesleys, together with two Vincents of No 430 Flight. In a reprisal attack on 18 October, three Gladiators of No 1 Sqn SAAF strafed Barentù airfield, destroying three *Falcos* of 412ª *Squadriglia.*

Italian troops based in Albania invaded Greece on 28 October. This badly organised operation against a country that Italy had previously enjoyed good relations with was ordered by Mussolini himself because he was determined to show his German allies that the Italian army could also gain fast and easy victories. When the campaign commenced, the only fighter unit available to cover the invasion was 160° *Gruppo Autonomo.* It was soon joined by 150° *Gruppo* from northern Italy and 24° *Gruppo*, equipped with G.50s. Opposing them were four *Mire Dioxes* (fighter squadrons) of the *Elleniki Vassiliki Aeroporia EVA* (Royal Hellenic Air Force), equipped with 36 PZL P.24s and nine Bloch MB.151s.

160° *Gruppo Autonomo* had detached one of its *squadriglie* – 395ª – to the advanced base of Berat with four G.50s. This unit was to operate autonomously, forming the core around which was built the new 154° *Gruppo Autonomo.* The other *squadriglie*, 393ª and 394ª, were equipped with nine CR.42s and 14 CR.32s, respectively. These units split their aircraft between the airfields at Koritza and Drenowa, in Albania.

On the morning of the 28th, Italian pilots were frequently

This CR.42, possibly from 365ª *Squadriglia,* 150° *Gruppo*, is seen at Argirocastro airfield in Albania in the autumn of 1940. Muddy conditions have forced the groundcrew to remove the fighter's wheel spats so as to prevent clogging (*Roberto Gentilli*)

Wearing his standard issue baggy flying overalls, Tenente Ranieri Carlo Piccolomini Clementini Adami strikes a pose for the camera outside the 92ª *Squadriglia* operations hut in North Africa in 1940. A nobleman from a famous family (he numbered two popes among his ancestors), Adami was also a veteran of the Spanish Civil War – he had served in an assault unit. Piccolomini claimed 7 and 12 shared victories during World War 2, one of which was achieved while flying the CR.42 on 15 October 1940 when he downed a No 208 Sqn Lysander between Sollum and Giarabub. This was Piccolomini's second victory of the war, his first having been claimed on 14 June when he was credited with shooting down a No 33 Sqn Gladiator while flying a CR.32. His unit (part of 8° *Gruppo*) re-equipped with CR.42s in early July. Later in the war Piccolomini transferred to 4° *Stormo*, and after the Armistice he and most other pilots in this unit joined the *Aeronautica Cobelligerante*. From 31 December 1944 until war's end Piccolomini commanded 4° *Stormo*. He remained in the *Aeronautica Militare Italiana* post-war (*Renato Zavattini*)

scrambled to intercept Greek reconnaissance aircraft. The first kill went to CR.42 pilot Tenente Mario Gaetano Carancini of 393ª *Squadriglia*, who intercepted a Henschel Hs 126 observation aircraft of 3 *Mira* and claimed to have damaged it. The aircraft was subsequently confirmed as having been shot down by advancing Italian troops.

Two days later, a mixed patrol of five CR.42s (again from 393ª *Squadriglia*) and two CR.32s had scrambled from Koritza in search of more Hs 126s that were flying repeated sorties over northwest Greece. Two reconnaissance machines were encountered over the frontline, and *Falco* pilot Sergent Maggiore Walter Rattichieri claimed to have shot one down, while Tenente Colonello Zanni heavily damaged the other. Both machines, again from 3 *Mira*, had in fact been destroyed.

October ended with the biggest air combat so far seen in the Mediterranean theatre. At 1315 hrs on the 31st over Mersa Matruh, in Egypt, nine Gladiators of No 112 Sqn and 12 Hurricanes from No 33 Sqn scrambled to intercept a mixed formation of 26 SM.79s escorted by 37 CR.42s drawn from 13° and 151° *Gruppi*. The Italian fighters, unable to closely escort the Savoias due to their lack of endurance, arrived over the target area independently to find the bombers already under attack by small groups of British fighters. In perfect visibility, and with the advantage of height and numbers, the *Falcos* bounced the Gladiators and Hurricanes and downed five of the former and two of the latter.

Looking at British records, and the reconstructed Operational Record Book of No 112 Sqn in particular, it appears that four of the five RAF biplanes lost were downed by engine failure, collisions with friendly aircraft or return fire from the bombers. Crosschecking British losses with Italian combat reports, it seems more likely that three of the Gladiators had indeed been shot down by the *Falcos*. The only CR.42 lost during the combat, piloted by Tenente Gianfranco Perversi of 13° *Gruppo*, had been seen to collide with the Gladiator it was chasing.

Honours for the day went to 13° *Gruppo* pilots Capitano Domenico Bevilacqua and to the now deceased Perversi. They were each credited with shooting down two Gladiators, while Tenente Guglielmo Chiarini shared in the destruction of a Hurricane with Sergente Francesco Nanin.

While 13° *Gruppo* fought the Gladiators, the Hurricanes of No 33 Sqn had been engaged by 368ª *Squadriglia* of 151° *Gruppo*. Sergente Maggiore Davide Colauzzi and Sergente Mario Turchi each claimed a fighter destroyed, while their leader, Capitano Bruno Locatelli, damaged a third. A short while later, Locatelli spotted a lone Gladiator over the coast. Opening fire with a short burst from close range, he saw the British fighter 'explode' in mid-air directly ahead of him. This may have been the No 112 Sqn machine of Flg Off R H Clark, who failed to return to base.

Capitano Bernardino Serafini, CO of 366ª *Squadriglia*, encountered five SM.79s in arrow formation as they headed away from the target, closely followed by a Hurricane. Flying at full throttle in an attempt to intercept the British fighter, Serafini could not prevent one of the Savoias being downed in flames. Eventually catching the Hurricane, he hit its fuselage and the fighter also went down – but not before Serafini had seen a second SM.79 engulfed in flames and sent to its destruction by the RAF fighter. The Italian had probably shot down Canadian Flg Off E K Leveille, who had just accounted for two SM.79s.

Finally, a sixth Gladiator was credited to Sergente Maggiore Roberto Marchi, who had attacked the fighter after it had been damaged by Serafini in the opening minutes of the combat.

Bernardino Serafini had gained a permanent commission in the air force in 1934, and he would spend his entire combat career with 151° *Gruppo*. After the victory on the 31st, he claimed two more Hurricanes destroyed in subsequent actions in the CR.42. It was men like him, mature permanent officers, carefully trained in the pre-war years, who initially served as *squadriglia* commanders during World War 2. They formed the backbone of the fighter arm, and gave sterling service in the opening stages of the conflict. When attrition reduced this well-trained force at an increasingly fast pace, the *Regia Aeronautica* demonstrated an inability to replace the missing veterans – but that all lay in the future.

Indeed, such losses seemed inconceivable in October 1940, which proved to be the most positive month yet for CR.42 units in terms of victories. Some 17 kills had been claimed for just two combat losses. The latter figure was due mainly to the less frequent appearance of British fighters in North Africa. The acquisition of combat experience by *Falco* pilots had also meant better tactical employment of the Fiat fighter when the enemy was encountered. This in turn resulted in the downing of modern bombers like the Blenheim in significant numbers. CR.42 pilots had also learned to avoid the low-level dogfights with Gladiators that had caused so many losses during the summer months in North Africa.

Following these successes in the autumn, the *Falco* was now being viewed with more respect by RAF pilots, as seven-kill Gladiator and Hurricane ace Flg Off R A Acworth recalled. 'The Hurricanes had strict orders to beat a hasty retreat if they met enemy aircraft in large numbers, as it was thought at the time that they would be "easy meat" for the more manoeuvrable CR.42s – the Gladiator's Italian opposite number.'

But *Falco* units would soon find themselves up against it once again in both North and East Africa as Commonwealth forces steadily built up their strength. In Libya, Nos 33 and 274 Sqns swapped their Gladiators for Hurricanes, the biplane fighters in turn being passed on to No 3 Sqn Royal Australian Air Force (RAF). In East Africa, Nos 1 (Gladiators) and 3 Sqns (Hurricanes) of the SAAF arrived in the frontline.

Moreover, the Air Fighting Development Unit (AFDU) in the UK was formulating better tactics that would allow Hurricane pilots to deal with the *Falco* more effectively. These evolved following mock combats between Hurricanes and Gladiators. It soon became obvious to the AFDU that Hurricane pilots had to avoid turning engagements with the CR.42, and make better use of their superior speed to break off and resume attacks at will.

For its part, the *Regia Aeronautica,* by opening up fronts in Greece and over the Channel, had dispersed its forces and reduced its reserves to almost zero. This in turn meant that the CR.42 units were in no position to repel the imminent Allied counterattack.

Pilots from 4° *Stormo* smile for the camera in front of a CR.32 at El Adem, in Cyrenaica, between September and November 1940. These men are, from left to right, Aldo Gon (one CR.42 victory), Giulio Reiner (three CR.42 victories in an overall tally of ten and 57 shared), Carlo Agnelli (one shared victory in the CR.42), Ezio Viglione (one in the CR.42 from a total of five and six shared), Armando Moresi (one probable in the CR.42) and Alvaro Querci (two shared in the CR.42 from a total of six and five shared) (*Fulvio Chianese – Associazione Culturale 4° Stormo di Gorizia*)

On the morning of 1 November 150° *Gruppo* flew into the Albanian capital of Tirana from its base at Turin Casell. The unit's 37 CR.42s, split between three *squadriglie*, were immediately separated, with the 12 machines assigned to 363ª *Squadriglia* being sent to Drenowa to join 160° *Gruppo*. At the same time 364ª *Squadriglia* transferred to Valona, where it operated as an autonomous unit until the 20th, and 365ª *Squadriglia*, with 13 fighters, moved to Argyrokastron. All three squadrons quickly commenced escort missions for Italian bombers sent on raids into Greece, and fighter patrols were also flown over the front.

On the 2nd, five fighters from 365ª *Squadriglia*, led by Capitano Giorgio Graffer, had taken off at 1100 hrs. After an uneventful reconnaissance of the Kalibaki area, the biplanes headed for Yanina, where, at 1130 hrs, two P.24s were spotted. Immediately attacked, both fighters were claimed as shot down by the *Falco* pilots. Several minutes later, two more PZLs were encountered and one was reportedly shot down. In fact, two of the three P.24s that 21 *Mira* had detached to Yanina had been lost, apparently in two separate combats.

Three hours later, over Salonika, 12 CR.42s of 363ª *Squadriglia*, led by Capitano Luigi Mariotti, reportedly intercepted 'eight PZL.27s' and attacked them. Two fighters were seen to fall in flames and two more reportedly behaved as if they were out of control. In fact there were only six P.24s of 22 *Mira* involved in this engagement, and the sole casualty was Sminagos Johannes Kyriazes, who crash-landed. Other sources suggest that Sminias Konstantinos Lambropoulos had to bail out, although there are records to suggest that his loss happened the following day. In return, however, the Greeks had downed two Cant Z.1007bis.

393ª *Squadriglia* also suffered a loss on 2 November when Sergente Pippo Ardesio was killed in his fighter when it was destroyed by a bomb blast at Koritza whilst scrambling to intercept Greek Blenheims.

On the 4th, two machines from 365ª *Squadriglia* intercepted a pair of reconnaissance aircraft east of Smolika mountain. Sottotenente Lorenzo Clerici, who usually flew as Graffer's wingman, claimed to have shot down one of them with the assistance of Sergente Domenico Facchini. The other was seen to escape, smoking heavily, and it was claimed as a probable. In fact both Greek Breguet XIXs of 2 Mira were lost, with one force-landing after it was hit by the Fiats and the other crashing in flames with the loss of unit CO, Episminagos Fridericos Katassos.

That same day in East Africa, CR.42s from 412ª *Squadriglia* clashed with three SAAF Gladiators during an early patrol over Metemma. Although bounced by four *Falcos*, the three South Africa pilots quickly turned the tables and claimed three CR.42s destroyed. Only one Fiat was lost, however, its pilot bailing out. The *Falco* pilots in turn claimed a solitary kill, but none of the Gladiators suffered as much as a scratch!

At dawn on 6 November the first British offensive of World War 2 commenced in East Africa with the shelling of the fort in the border town of Gallabat. The aim of this campaign was to capture the fort, which was at the heart of the Italian defences in Sudan. The offensive was to be covered by Wellesleys and Vincents, together with all available fighters – the Gladiators of both No 1 Sqn SAAF and No 112 Sqn's 'K' Flight.

Using their height advantage to full effect, CR.42s of 412ª *Squadriglia* (led by Capitano Raffi) bounced a 'vic' of three RAF Gladiators from

'K' Flight that were covering the advancing troops east of Metemma. All of them were shot down. No 1 Sqn SAAF then tried to intervene, scrambling from its base at Azoza, but it too lost two more fighters. Unit CO Maj Schalk van Schalkwyk was killed and future ace Capt Boyle, who had tried to help his commander by attacking the whole Italian formation, was forced to crash-land when his fighter was badly damaged.

This one-sided action firmly established Italian air superiority over the area. Immediately, waves of Caproni bombers started to attack, finally forcing the Commonwealth troops to retreat.

In the early afternoon, five more Gladiators rose to challenge the Fiats, and K7977 was lost. The Italian fighters had suffered no losses, even if some aircraft had been damaged in combat. It is known that Tenente Visintini claimed three kills during the clashes. Together with the air battle of 31 October over Mersa Matruh, these actions in the defence of Gallabat demonstrated that Africa-based CR.42 units now understood how best to cope with the Gladiator using their superior vertical speed.

Sadly, things were rather different over the Channel, however, where, two months later than planned, the Italian fighters were finally to be tested in combat. The date fixed for the ill-fated Operation *Cinzano* was 11 November, and the target was the Essex port town of Harwich. The attack was to be carried out in the early afternoon by ten BR.20Ms of 43° *Stormo*. The mission had been carefully planned, with five Z.1007bis simulating a raid on the same target to draw British fighters away. Meanwhile, 20° *Gruppo* with its G.50s was to sweep the same general area, and 18° *Gruppo*, with no less than 40 aircraft, was to escort the bombers in what was supposed to be a safe ratio of four fighters for each BR.20M. But everything started to go wrong from the very beginning.

The Cants failed to deceive the defenders and the G.50s encountered thick cloud at 11,375 ft that they were unable to fly through, forcing them to turn back. One of the BR.20Ms also had to return early, while another with engine trouble pressed on behind the main force. This elongated the formation so that the distance between the first trio of bombers and this last machine was almost two miles! It would be impossible for the CR.42s to escort them effectively. Finally, weather conditions worsened, blinding the *Falco* pilots in their open cockpits.

Fighters from no fewer than four RAF squadrons were vectored to intercept this raid. At least two Hurricanes from No 249 Sqn, nine Hurricanes of No 257 Sqn, seven Hurricanes from No 46 Sqn and a Spitfire II from No 41 Sqn were able to engage the Italian formation. After an extremely confused dogfight in worsening weather, the British pilots returned without loss, claiming to have shot down all the BR.20Ms, together with five CR.42s. They also claimed many probables. In actuality, four bombers had been destroyed and two badly damaged.

For the *Falco* pilots the mission had been a disaster. Unable to protect their charges from the much faster Hurricanes that suddenly appeared out of the clouds, they tried to reciprocate this tactic as best they could in an engagement that resembled a game of hide-and-seek. The following, anonymous, report from one of the returning pilots reveals the sheer extent of their disorientation, and fantastical kill claiming;

'We were limping along at a height of between 21,100-22,800 ft. There were scattered clouds over the target when the CO, who had

Maresciallo Giuseppe Ruzzin of 85ª *Squadriglia*, 18° *Gruppo* is seen in CR.42 '85-9' at Ursel during the *CAI* campaign. Ruzzin was born in Spresiano, near Treviso, on 25 April 1916, and had served in the *XXIII Gruppo Asso di Bastoni* of the *Aviazione Legionaria* during the Spanish Civil War, claiming four individual and six shared victories. Returning to Italy in 1938, he was granted a permanent commission in the air force and transferred to 3° *Stormo*. Ruzzin participated in the first combats over Provence and was credited with three shared victories. He claimed a Hurricane destroyed in the Harwich area on 11 November 1940 during a one-sided combat with RAF fighters from Nos 46, 249 and 257 Sqns. The veteran ace survived the war (*Giuseppe Ruzzin via Gianandrea Bussi*)

CR.42 '95-12' of 95ª *Squadriglia*, 18° *Gruppo*, sits in a camouflaged, and damp, dispersal pen at Ursel with two other *Falcos* in November 1940 (*Giorgio Apostolo*)

probably seen the enemy fighters, dived. We followed swiftly. A Hurricane appeared in front of me, coming from the left. I fired at it but my guns jammed. We fought in a space between the clouds, then it ran away. I saw a CR.42 below me followed by a British fighter. The Fiat pulled up and escaped. I was in a position to fire, but only my 7.7 mm weapon was working. The Hurricane entered a cloud. The combat lasted five minutes. We were always above the Hurricanes, and I saw many of them nose-diving, leaving trails of smoke. We ended up scattered around the sky over the target. We knew the British losses only later thanks to the German HQ. From my logbook I see that we were credited with nine confirmed and four probable victories.'

Although the losses suffered over the target area had been bad, things got even worse for the *Falco* units on the return leg of the mission. The operation had started with a 40-minute delay caused by technical problems with the bombers. On the way to England it had appeared evident to all the CR.42 pilots that they did not have enough fuel to complete the mission and return safely. Nevertheless, the *squadriglia* commanders decided to press on. Following the attack on Harwich, the returning pilots encountered cloud over Belgium that extended from 19,500 ft down to 2300 ft or less. Low on fuel, and lacking radio and other navigational aids, the *Falco* pilots had to land where they could.

In the end three CR.42s failed to return, with two pilots captured and one killed, although two of them were not lost to enemy action. Two more machines were destroyed in crash-landings. One of the latter had been previously damaged by the Hurricanes to confirm the second of the five RAF claims. A further 17 *Falcos* were obliged to force-land far from their bases, five of them being heavily damaged in the process.

This ill-fated mission provided the basis for a well-orchestrated propaganda campaign that culminated in the British ridiculing the Italian pilots as 'macaroni airmen' flying obsolete aircraft. But the returning RAF pilots, seasoned veterans who had already encountered the best Luftwaffe units during the summer of 1940, noted in their combat reports that their adversaries' biplanes were difficult to keep in their gunsights. One reported, 'We made tight turns, climbing turns and half rolls until it seemed we would never stop. The Italians could certainly fly!'

In the Balkans, the first week of November saw Italian troops

CR.42 '95-6' of 95ª *Squadriglia*, 18° *Gruppo* came to grief upon its return to Belgian following the *CAI's* disastrous combat debut on 11 November 1940 (*Giorgio Apostolo*)

starting to run into stiff opposition from the Greek army. The RAF had also prepared an expeditionary force to assist the Greeks, whose modest air arm was rapidly tiring. Blenheim Is of Nos 30 and 84 Sqns were to supplement the *EVA*, together with a detachment of Wellingtons from No 70 Sqn. The Gladiators of No 80 Sqn and more Blenheim Is from No 211 Sqn would soon join them.

Three CR.42's from 85ª *Squadriglia*, 18° *Gruppo* are seen on the wing in late 1940. '85-4' was flown by Sottotenente Peppo Re during the 11 November mission to Harwich. Re escaped unharmed from the British fighters' onslaught, but he found himself low on fuel by the time he reached Belgium and had to make a force-landing near Dunderlewe, where his fighter overturned (*Roberto Gentilli*)

The aircraft of No 30 Sqn were the first to encounter the Italians during a bombing mission to the port of Valona on 6 November. Having attacked the town's airfield, three Blenheims were hunted down by a trio of CR.42s from 394ª *Squadriglia* that had scrambled from the base. All three were badly holed, and Capitano Nicola Magaldi claimed one destroyed, but the Blenheims made it back to Eleusis. The following day, over Valona, five CR.42s of 364ª *Squadriglia* and two G.50s of 395ª *Squadriglia* shared in the destruction of a pair of Wellingtons.

On the 14th the Greek Army launched a counteroffensive that not only blunted the Italian invasion, it sent Mussolini's troops streaming back into Albania. To sustain this operation, the *EVA* put up a maximum effort against the airfields of Drenowa and Koritza. Two Blenheims from 32 *Mira* and two Fairey Battles from 33 *Mira* attacked the latter airfield at 0945hrs. One Blenheim was destroyed by a direct AAA hit, while the other was pursued by two fighters from 393ª *Squadriglia* piloted by Tenente Torquato Testerini and Sergente Maggiore Walter Rattichieri, who had scrambled at 0910 hrs. Testerini, who left his prey once he had expended all his ammunition, initially claimed a probable, but Ratticchieri stubbornly followed the Blenheim and witnessed it belly-land close to its base at Larissa to confirm the victory.

Rattichieri then spotted what he believed were two Hurricanes taking off from the same airfield. He attacked one of them and claimed to have shot it down. The 'Hurricanes' were in fact two Battles of 33 *Mira,* one of which sustained severe damage, although it returned to base.

Nine P.24s from 23 *Mira* had taken off from Larissa shortly after Rattichieri's encounter with the Battles and headed for the frontline. First to encounter the Greeks was the lone CR.42 of Sergente Augusto Manetti of 363ª *Squadriglia*, who had scrambled from Drenowa at 0935 hrs to intercept Blenheims. He was reportedly bounced by 'six PZLs' and forced to bail out. At 0950 hrs two more fighters from the same unit were scrambled, followed ten minutes later by a further pair of Fiats (one of which was flown by future ace Sottotenente Ugo Drago). Finally, at 1015 hrs, two more CR.42s, led by Sottotenente Romeo Della Costanza, departed Drenowa. The three sections independently encountered three groups of three, nine and three P.24s, respectively. Drago's section claimed one victory, firing a total of 1000 rounds of ammunition, while Della Costanza's was credited with another, having fired 345 rounds.

About an hour later, at 1055 hrs, the last Italian fighter departed when Tenente Mario Gaetano Carancini took off from Koritza in his 393ª *Squadriglia* machine. It is possible that he encountered the same Greek formation of three 'PZL P.24As' that Della Costanza had run into. Carancini claimed another enemy fighter destroyed, although his aircraft was damaged in the process. At 1140 hrs three more CR.42s from 363ª and 393ª *Squadriglie* took off to intercept a group of six PZL P.24s from 23 *Mira*. This time it was the Greek pilots who prevailed, killing Sottotenente Ernesto Trevisi and forcing Sergente Vittorio Pirchio of 393ª *Squadriglia* to crash-land back at his base. The Italians were unable to claim any victories to balance these losses.

Raids continued throughout the day, and when Greek and Italian fighters clashed during the afternoon, Sottotenente Drago, who had taken off at 1325 hrs with two wingmen, bounced a formation of ten P.24s. Three Greek fighters were seen to fall away trailing smoke, and they were claimed as shot down by the CR.42 pilots. Two Fiats were damaged, however. Greek losses for 14 November are not known in detail, but some sources reported that during the day four fighters from 23 *Mira* were damaged and may have force-landed.

CR.42s from an unidentified unit also intercepted three Blenheims from No 84 Sqn over Koritza on the 14th, shooting down L1389 and L1387 and damaging the third machine.

The following day, *EVA* consolidated 21 and 22 *Mira* and transferred the combined unit to a forward advanced airfield to support the army as it pushed on towards Albania. Encounters over the frontline resulted in another victory for 393ª *Squadriglia* when, at around 1500 hrs, L1120 of No 30 Sqn was shot down in flames by Sergente Maggiore Rattichieri. A further victory was attributed to 363ª *Squadriglia* later that same day when the unit shot down a Battle from 33 *Mira* and severely damaged a second aircraft. Finally, 393ª *Squadriglia* pilot Sottotenente Maurizio Nicolis Di Robilant attacked three Battles whilst escorting a Meridionali Ro.37bis army cooperation aircraft from 72° *Gruppo*.

Spotting the bombers attacking targets near Koritza, Di Robilant claimed to have shot all three Battles down in just four minutes. His claims were confirmed by the observer in the Ro.37bis, and his achievement lauded in the Italian press, even if the *EVA's* actual losses (one Battle destroyed and a second aircraft damaged) were less severe.

With many of the RAF squadrons in North Africa preparing for a transfer to Greece in early November, the *Regia Aeronautica* failed to encounter Allied aircraft again until the 16th, when six CR.42s from 151° *Gruppo* (led by Tenente Mario Ferrero) intercepted a No 208 Sqn Lysander as it was photographing Mektila camp from 18,000 ft. Whilst Flg Off Benson vainly tried to shake off his pursuers, his gunner, Sgt Phillips, put up a valiant defence until his gun jammed. By then he had downed the CR.42 of Tenente Sacchetti, who was killed. The Lysander eventually crash-landed not far from the downed *Falco*.

The CR.42s again took on Greek P.24s on 18 November when, in two separate combats over Koritza, the pilots of 393ª *Squadriglia* claimed to have shot down six Greek fighters. The first action developed during the morning after two *Falcos* had scrambled at 1005 hrs. Tenente Carancini and Sergente Biolcati reported encountering three PZLs, and they claimed to have shot down one apiece. Early in the afternoon, three machines from the same *squadriglia* took off at 1316 hrs and engaged four PZLs. The Italian pilots claimed to have downed all of the Greek machines, and stated that three airmen were seen to bail out and land inside friendly territory. Sergente Maggiore Arturo Bonato claimed two victories and Tenente Testerini and Sergente Minella one each.

Greek sources show that Yposminagos Costantinos Yanikostas of 22 *Mira* was killed, as was Sminias Gregorios Valcanas of 23 *Mira*, although he was reported to have rammed an Italian bomber. Yposminagos Corneleus Kotrones of 22 *Mira* was wounded and force-landed. According to other sources, Episminias Dimitrakopoulos bailed out of his damaged fighter, while Anthiposminagos Giannikostas made it back to base. In return, the Greeks claimed two kills – no CR.42s were lost.

Amongst the *Falco* pilots to enjoy success was 25-year-old Mario Gaetano Carancini, who had scored his third individual victory of the campaign. He would subsequently receive a *Medaglia d'Argento al valor militare* for his achievements over Greece.

At 1410 hrs on the 19th, nine Gladiators of No 80 Sqn's 'B' Flight, led by Sqn Ldr W J Hickey, finally reached Eleusis following a nine-day transit from Egypt via Crete. Immediately led north to Trikkala by three P.24s, the British pilots reported encountering 'small enemy formations', which they attacked. They had bounced four 160° *Gruppo Falcos* and two G.50s of 24° *Gruppo*. The Fiat fighter flown by Sergente Maggiore Natale Viola of 363ª *Squadriglia* was reportedly attacked by '20 Glosters and three PZLs' and shot down. Viola had probably fallen victim to Flt Lt Pattle, who 'made ace' with two CR.42 claims on this date. A G.50 was also downed after its pilot single-handedly attacked six Gladiators.

The eight remaining combat-ready Fiats of 160° *Gruppo* were hastily scrambled at 1525 hrs (led by Capitano Arcangeletti) from the forward airfield of Koritza in an effort to help in the fight against the RAF Gladiators, but they were attacked while still climbing by the aggressive British pilots. Maresciallo Giuseppe Salvadori of 363ª *Squadriglia* and Sergente Maggiore Arturo Bonato of 393ª *Squadriglia* perished, while Sergente Maggiore Rattichieri, also from 393ª *Squadriglia*, was hit early on in the fight and wounded in both legs.

The jubilant British pilots landed at Trikkala and claimed six CR.42s and three G.50s destroyed at the modest cost of one aircraft damaged. Flying the latter machine was Plt Off Vincent Stuckey, who was wounded after being attacked by two CR.42s. Sqn Ldr Hickey was able to save him by driving the *Falcos* away and then escorting him back to base. It seems that Stuckey, who had become an ace in the early stages of the engagement with his fourth and fifth victories, was wounded by Sergente Luciano Tarantini and Capitano Arcangeletti. The Italian pair claimed one victory and one probable, respectively.

This one-sided action resulted in the loss of four pilots, which came as a huge shock to the Italians. It also caused the CR.42 units to change tactics by halting the small patrols that had characterised the first weeks of fighter operations in Greece.

19 November also saw Gladiators of No 3 Sqn RAAF tangle with CR.42s for the first time over Egypt. Six *Falcos* of 13° *Gruppo*, led by Tenente Chiarini, were escorting a further 12 ground strafing CR.42s

from the same unit when they intercepted four Australian Gladiators flying one of their first missions. They quickly shot down the unit CO, Sqn Ldr P Heath, who was killed, and damaged Flt Lt Pelly's fighter so badly that he was forced to land with a dead engine. Chiarini was credited with his fourth victory following this combat, which saw both sides badly over-claiming – the Australian pilots were credited with three kills and a probable and the Italians six kills and two probables!

The following day Gladiator-equipped No 112 Sqn evened up the score when, over Sidi Barrani, it shot down three CR.42s of 9° *Gruppo*, resulting in the loss of Sergente Putzu of 97ª *Squadriglia* and Sottotenente Agnelli of 96ª *Squadriglia*. No RAF losses were reported.

The next action involving the CR.42 occurred in Greece on 22 November when *Falcos* from 160° *Gruppo* shot down an Hs126 of 3 *Mira* over Kapetista whilst escorting SM.79s. That same day a Battle of No 11 Sqn SAAF was destroyed by fighters from 413ª *Squadriglia* over Kismayu, in Italian Somaliland.

The CR.42 was now active on all war fronts to which the *Regia Aeronautica* had been committed, and on 23 November there were more losses for 18° *Gruppo* when it again tried to 'mix it' with the hardened veterans of RAF Fighter Command on the Channel front. This time 29 fighters took off at 1250 hrs for a free sweep over the southeastern coast of England. The Fiat pilots flew half-frozen in the open cockpits of their aircraft at a height of 21,000 ft, but to no avail. British fighters were sighted flying about 5000 ft above them. They were in fact Spitfire IIAs of No 603 Sqn, and they dived on the Italians in a devastating firing pass, before disengaging. Five CR.42s failed to return to base, two pilots being killed when their fighters plunged into the sea. The remaining three were wounded when they force-landed prior to reaching their base.

The pilots of 18° *Gruppo* were in turn credited with five victories, although only one Spitfire was reported to have been slightly damaged. It was painfully clear that the days of the *CAI* were definitely over. There were no further missions over England, and 18° *Gruppo* was ordered back to Italy on 20 December.

A trio of CR.42s from an unidentified unit close up for the camera. Note that two of the fighters have tricoloured propeller spinners – a decoration adopted by several units in 1940-41 (*Giorgio Apostolo*)

While its *Falcos* were being mauled by the RAF over southern England, 23° *Gruppo* (18° *Gruppo's* sister unit) had put up 18 CR.42s to escort ten SM.79s sent to raid Malta's Ta'Qali airfield on 23 November. This was first action of note for the *Falcos* on this front in a number of weeks. Eight Hurricanes of No 261 Sqn scrambled to intercept them, but without success. The Italian pilots were credited with four victories, however, the successful claimants being Capitano Guido Bobba of 74ª *Squadriglia*, Tenente Claudio Solaro and Sergente Pardino Pardini of 70ª *Squadriglia* and several pilots from

75ª *Squadriglia*. In reality, only Flt Lt H F R Bradbury's Hurricane had been badly hit, obliging the pilot to force-land at Luqa airfield. No other loss or damage was sustained by either side.

The following day, Tenente Monti and Sergente Gasperoni from 75ª *Squadriglia* claimed a lone Wellington shot down into the sea 30 miles from Malta. On the 26th, the same unit despatched Capitano Guido Bobba on a reconnaissance mission over Malta, accompanied by Tenente Giuseppe Beccaria and Sergente Manlio Tarantino. Flying at high altitude, Bobba was affected by a lack of oxygen just as two Hurricanes that had approached undetected attacked his patrol. Regaining consciousness after he had lost height, Bobba saw a Hurricane cross in front of him. He reacted immediately by opening fire and the fighter was seen to fall away engulfed in smoke and flames. Bobba had downed Sgt Dennis Ashton of No 261 Sqn. Moments earlier the latter had accounted for the Fiat flown by Beccaria. Both pilots were killed.

That same day in East Africa, 412ª *Squadriglia* shot down newly arrived Blenheim IV R3593, which was flying as part of a six-aircraft formation from No 14 Sqn that had been sent to bomb Nefasit. This unit had converted to the Bristol bomber after losing 12 Wellesleys in the first five months of war – many to CR.42s.

Following the shocking reversal suffered on 19 November at the hands of No 80 Sqn, the *Regia Aeronautica* had started to put up bigger formations over Greece in an effort to counter the RAF Gladiator threat. CR.42s and clashed with the unit once again on the morning of the 27th, when 364ª *Squadriglia* of 150° *Gruppo* flew three patrols with nine fighters and a fourth with six. The second mission commenced at 1100 hrs, when Capitano Nicola Magaldi took off from Valona. Spotting some unidentified bombers, he and the two pilots in his section went to investigate, but they lost touch with the rest of the formation.

Minutes later they were surprised by nine Gladiators from No 80 Sqn that were patrolling in the same area. Two CR.42s were claimed as shot down by the RAF pilots, and Magaldi was indeed killed. However, Sergente Negri managed to return to base in his heavily damaged *Falco*.

The Fiats of 412ª Squadriglia had better luck in East Africa on the 27th when they shot down Hardy K4311 of No 237 Sqn over the Metemma area, killing the gunner.

Late November also saw CR.42 units based in the Mediterranean engage the Fleet Air Arm for the first time as the Italian fleet clashed with the Royal Navy's Force 'H' off the Sardinian coast in the Battle of Cape Spartivento. To cover Italian bombers attacking the British ships, 3° *Gruppo Autonomo* put up the few CR.42s that had been assigned to 153ª and 154ª *Squadriglie* – 155ª *Squadriglia* was still flying CR.32s.

At 1430 hrs on 27 November, two of seven patrolling Fulmars from 808 Naval Air Squadron (NAS), embarked in HMS *Ark Royal*, were bounced by five CR.42s led by future ace Capitano Giorgio Tugnoli. Minutes earlier the Fulmars had attacked SM.79s sent to bomb Force 'H'. The Fiat pilots claimed five kills, although they only managed to shoot down N1941. During the return flight, probably low on fuel, Sergente Lucato was posted missing. The following day it was 23° *Gruppo's* turn to fight Fulmars when six aircraft from HMS *Illustrious'* 805 and 806 NASs intercepted a similar number of CR.42s on a

Capitano Guido Bobba, CO of 74ª *Squadriglia*, is seen here trussed up in an Italian cork life-vest – pilots nicknamed these 'sausages'. A skilled and aggressive leader who had claimed an aerial victory during the Spanish Civil War, Bobba was credited with 3 at 1 shared victories in the CR.42. The first of these came after he fought the Hal Far Fighter Flight Hurricane of Plt Off Sudgen on 13 July 1940. The second came on 23 November in combat with No 261 Sqn Hurricanes and the third was claimed three days later following a clash with the same unit. In December 1940 23° *Gruppo* was transferred from Sicily to Tripoli, and on the 26th Bobba was killed in combat with Gladiators from No 3 Sqn RAAF. He was subsequently awarded a posthumous *Medaglia d'Argento al Valor Militare* (*Nicola Malizia*)

This photograph shows one of the few CR.42s assigned to 3° *Gruppo Autonomo* during the autumn of 1940. It lacks tactical markings, although a white '4' is visible on the rear of the fuselage, to the right of which is the famous 'grinning devil' unit insignia. The start of the war found this *Gruppo* based on Sardinia, from where it took part in the Battle of Cape Spartivento on 27 November 1940 (*Robert Gentilli*)

reconnaissance mission to Malta. The CR.42 flown by Sergente Maggiore Arnaldo Sala was downed by 806 NAS ace Sub Lt Stan Orr and two more fighters damaged.

The 28th also saw plenty of action over Malta itself, when 16 CR.42s again from 23° *Gruppo* escorted Italian Ju 87s that had been sent to attack a newly arrived British supply convoy. Intercepted by Hurricanes, the *Falco* pilots (including Capitano Guido Bobba) claimed four British fighters destroyed. There are no RAF records to corroborate this action, however. The same *Gruppo* escorted SM.79s sent to attack shipping off Malta later that same day, and Sergente Maggiore Marzocca of 74ª *Squadriglia* claimed a Hurricane destroyed.

The final action in a hectic month for the *Falco* units ended in tragedy for the *Regia Aeronautica*. Again, this engagement took place on 28 November, but this time the location was Delvinakion, in Greece. At 0845 hrs, 150° *Gruppo* had sent aloft a strong formation of ten fighters from 364ª and 365ª *Squadriglie* in search of the No 80 Sqn Gladiators that had caused so many losses since arriving in-theatre on 18 November. The Italian biplanes were led by CR.42 ace Capitano Giorgio Graffer.

Twenty minutes after take-off, Graffer spotted a formation of three Gladiators flying below him and he immediately attacked them. The three Gladiators were from 'A' Flight of No 80 Sqn, which was patrolling over the front. That day, the RAF pilots had adopted a new and more open formation, and three more machines, led by future ace Flt Lt 'Tap' Jones, were flying three miles behind the first trio.

Graffer's machines had just started their attack when they were surprised by the second 'vic' led by Jones, which intervened with deadly effect. After a ferocious dogfight three *Falcos* failed to return. Graffer was one of those lost, as was Sergente Corrado Mignani, who had been seen to collide with Gladiator N5812 flown by Flg Off H U Sykes (both men perished). The final machine lost was flown by Sergente Achille Pacini, who returned to base on foot that night in a state of shock. Additionally, Maresciallo Guglielmo Bacci and Sergente Arrigo Zotti were wounded, although they were able to make it back to Valona.

The British formation did not escape unscathed, however, as aside from the loss of Sykes, Flt Lt Jones was badly wounded. Indeed, only the Gladiator of Sgt D S Gregory emerged from the clash unscathed. The Italians claimed three victories (later raised to four), one of them apparently being credited to Zotti – the RAF pilots claimed seven kills and two probables. Graffer's body was identified by retreating Italian troops, but it was not possible to recover it until June 1941. He was immediately awarded a posthumous *Medaglia d'Oro al valor militare*, and similar decorations followed for Magaldi and Ernesto Trevisi.

Greek fighters were again encountered by 160° *Gruppo* on 3 December, the unit having put up a formation of 18 CR.42s at 0845 hrs. The Italian machines were led by the unit's new CO, Maggiore Oscar Molinari, who had succeeded Tenente Colonello Eugenio Leotta on 24 November. As they patrolled over Koritza a formation of six P.24s was sighted and four were reportedly shot down. Molinari filed one claim and Sergente Maggiore Luciano Tarantini another. At least one of the Polish-built fighters, flown by Yposminagos Konstantinos Tsetsas of 23 *Mira*, was lost during this combat.

The following day 150° *Gruppo* again encountered British fighters when a formation of 15 CR.42s, led by the *Gruppo* CO, Tenente Colonello Rolando Pratelli, was attacked by nine Gladiators from No 80 Sqn and four from the recently arrived No 112 Sqn – the unit had transferred in a detachment from Egypt. The combat proceeded in a similar way to that on 28 November until Pratelli, diving on six Gladiators that had been sighted below him, spotted two additional formations of British fighters 3250 ft above him. He immediately aborted the attack and climbed towards the RAF machines.

By then the latter aircraft, led by Flt Lt Pattle, were following their leader in a diving attack on the Italian formation – Pattle's favoured tactic in the Gladiator. A confused dogfight ensued that also included ten G.50s of 154° *Gruppo*, which had been orbiting at higher altitude. Two CR.42s failed to return, resulting in the deaths of Tenente Alberto Triolo and Sottotenent Carlo Penna from 364ª *Squadriglia* – five more *Falcos* were damaged. In return, the Gladiator of No 80 Sqn CO Sqn Ldr W J Hickey was so badly shot up that it had to be written off, and two more were damaged. The CR.42 pilots made two claims and the G.50 unit one. The returning British pilots reported that on this occasion the Italians had avoided manoeuvring with the Gladiators in the horizontal plane, sticking rigidly to climbing or diving attacks instead.

4 December also saw 412ª *Squadriglia* continue its domination of the skies in East Africa when the unit downed Blenheim IV R2770 of No 14 Sqn as it attempted a solo reconnaissance mission over Eritrea. This may have been yet another victory for ranking *Falco* ace Tenente Mario Visintini, who, in a letter home during this period, wrote;

'On 26 November I intercepted a formation of six fast Blenheims, shooting down one (R3593 of No 14 Sqn) and scattering the others, which failed to reach their target. On the 4th I intercepted a Blenheim reconnaissance aeroplane and "fixed it" (R2770 of No 14 Sqn).'

Up to that point the Italian ace had accounted for at least nine Commonwealth aircraft.

On the 6th, 412ª *Squadriglia* shot down one of three Wellesleys from No 47 Sqn that had targeted the village and fort at Burie. The CR.42 pilots erroneously claimed all of the aircraft destroyed.

The following evening, Malta-based Wellingtons of No 148 Sqn attacked Italian rear areas in the Tripoli region, losing two of their number to the CR.42s of the local point defence sections. The day's hero was Sergente Vito Rinaldi, who claimed to have shot down one of the bombers and possibly damaged two others.

7 December was not a good day for the RAF bomber force in Greece either, as three of No 84 Sqn's Blenheim Is were lost in an attack on Valona harbour. L1381, L8455 and L8457 were intercepted and shot down by a section of three CR.42s from 365ª *Squadriglia*, led by Sottotenente Lorenzo Clerici. He claimed two confirmed and one probable victory after the wreckage of only two Blenheims was found.

Aside from being a very capable fighter pilot, Tenente Giorgio Graffer also happened to be a famous mountaineer pre-war. By the time the conflict started he was CO of 365ª *Squadriglia*, 150° *Gruppo*. On the night of 13/14 August 1940 he intercepted a bomber over Turin in a CR.42 that lacked both a radio and nightfighting equipment. After unsuccessfully attacking the bomber with his guns, he deliberately rammed Whitley V P4965 of No 10 Sqn – it later crashed into the Channel whilst trying to make it back to England. Graffer went on to claim four more victories with the CR.42 over Greece prior to being killed whilst dogfighting with No 80 Sqn Gladiators on 28 November 1940. Graffer was awarded a posthumous *Medaglia d'Oro al Valor Militare* (*Casucci via Andrea Fabianelli*)

DEFEAT IN NORTH AFRICA

At 0700 hrs on 9 December 1940, with the Italian Army heavily committed to halting the Greek offensive in Albania, the British commander-in-chief in the Middle East, Gen Archibald Wavell, launched his first counteroffensive against enemy troops entrenched around Sidi el-Barrani, in Egypt. An attack launched from Sudan and Kenya against Italian East Africa was soon to follow. The drive on Sidi el-Barrani, codenamed Operation *Compass*, had been planned as a limited offensive, but its results were to be beyond expectations. The Italian 10th Army and its air component, V^a^ *Squadra Aerea*, were crushed.

Operation *Compass* saw the heaviest air fighting yet seen in the Mediterranean theatre. The first four days of the battle were characterised by bad weather and sand storms, which restricted air activity. Unperturbed by the conditions, British armoured brigades defeated the frontline Italian divisions to quickly reach the Libyan border.

Some of the earliest clashes of the offensive took place on the morning of the 9th between 151° *Gruppo* and the Blenheim IVs of No 113 Sqn. The latter unit lost T2073, possibly to CR.42 ace Guglielmo Chiarini, who had only recently returned to 151° *Gruppo* – he had served with the unit pre-war. Two Blenheim Is from No 45 Sqn (L1534 and L6663), which had attacked Menastir, also force-landed following an encounter with a patrol from 8° *Gruppo*. There was an early loss for the *Falco* units too, however, when the CR.42 of Sergente Francesco Nanin of 82^a^ *Squadriglia* was shot down by a Hurricane from No 33 Sqn, probably piloted by Canadian ace Flg Off Vernon Woodward.

The initial struggle for air superiority over the frontline developed during the afternoon when 19 *Falcos* of 9° *Gruppo*, led by Maggiore Botto, were intercepted by five Hurricanes from No 274 Sqn. There may have been others, possibly from No 33 Sqn, which employed the AFDU's hit and run tactics for the first time over this sector. The results were impressive. Despite their numerical inferiority, the Hurricane pilots shot down four CR.42s. One crashed in flames, its pilot bailing out into captivity, and three others made force-landings. The British reported suffering no losses, and victories were claimed by Sqn Ldr 'Paddy' Dunn, Flt Lts John Lapsley and Peter Wykeham-Barnes, Plt Off Ernest Mason and Flg Off Thomas Patterson – all future aces in North Africa.

The day's fighting ended with a Hurricane of No 33 Sqn crash-landing, possibly under the combined fire of Capitano Locatelli, Tenente Furio Lauri and two other pilots of 368^a^ *Squadriglia*.

Like most of the Hurricane pilots that enjoyed great success on the opening day of *Compass*, Flt Lt Lapsley was a pre-war aviator with vast experience in biplane and monoplane fighters. Indeed, he had initially flown Gladiators in combat with No 80 Sqn prior to switching to

Hurricanes. He had six SM.79 kills to his name by the time he downed the first of his eventual five CR.42 victories on 9 December. Lapsley made the following comments about the *Falco* in relation to RAF fighters of the day when interviewed by historian Chris Shores in the 1960s;

'The Gladiator and the CR.42 were very evenly matched. The CR.42, however, had a constant speed airscrew, while that of the Gladiator was still fixed pitch. This gave the CR.42 a significantly better rate of climb, which the Italians always used to their advantage when they wanted to disengage from combat. The constant speed airscrew also gave the CR.42 a rather higher flat-out diving speed. However, the Gladiator was more manoeuvrable, and its four 0.303-in Browning machine gun armament was better than the 12.7 mm cannons of the CR.42. In this context, there is no doubt that the Italians were mistaken in arming these guns exclusively with explosive ammunition. This detonated on impact with virtually no penetration, and there is no doubt whatever that both Wykeham-Barnes and Pattle would have been killed when they were shot down had this not been so.

'The Hurricane was of course vastly superior to the CR.42 in both speed and armament, and it also carried armoured plating. This aircraft quickly gave us air supremacy. However, the manoeuvrability of the CR.42s in comparison with the Hurricanes made them difficult to shoot down once they had seen you, unless they were foolish enough to endeavour to disengage by diving. Most of us fought many engagements with CR.42s which developed into an unending series of inconclusive, but very frightening, head-on attacks as the Italian fighters turned to meet us each time as we came in.'

Bad weather initially limited activity on 10 December, but the situation on the ground appeared so serious for the Italians that the *Regia Aeronautica* was ordered to make an all-out effort to attack British vehicles using whatever aircraft were available. This forced the CR.42 pilots to fly through sand storms that sometimes topped off at 3350 ft. The same conditions also dictated that they make their strafing attacks far closer to the ground than was normal. Their fighters' sand filters were not effective in such an environment, and in a matter of days this would lead to a complete *squadriglia* being out of action due to powerplant problems, as had happened in June.

That morning, Hurricanes of No 33 Sqn surprised a formation from 8° *Gruppo* while it was landing after a defensive patrol. Sottotenente Nunzio De Fraia was shot down and wounded.

During the afternoon a patrol of four Gladiators from No 3 Sqn RAAF was able to use the weather conditions to surprise seven *Falcos* from 367ª *Squadriglia* that were strafing over Tummar West. Sergente Gino Bogoni was shot down and captured – the Australians claimed three kills. The formation from 367ª *Squadriglia* was supposed to have been covered by 14 more CR.42s from the *gruppo*, but the visibility was so poor that they were unable to see what was going on below them.

While returning to base, Capitano Locatelli, accompanied by Tenente Zuffi, Sergente Colauzzi and two more pilots, attacked a lone Hurricane that was strafing the road between Sidi el-Barrani and Buq-Buq. Although clearly hit, the British fighter, flown by South Africa Lt Fisches of No 33 Sqn, was seen to escape. It was claimed as damaged, although the RAF reported that Fisches had failed to return from an evening patrol over the road west of Sidi el-Barrani. A second No 33 Sqn Hurricane is known to have force-landed that day, but at an unknown time.

Dyson's Record

11 December was a big day for No 33 Sqn's Flg Off Charles Dyson. Flying a solo mission between Bardia and Sollum, he sighted a formation of six Breda Ba.65 ground attack aircraft escorted by five CR.42s. Diving after them, Dyson claimed to have shot all the biplane fighters down in just a matter of minutes. Then, on his way home, he encountered two more *Falcos*. Dyson reported;

'I was over Sollum Bay. There, I saw two more CRs making their way homeward. The leader saw me manoeuvring and they parted. Both the leader and I stall-turned, and we faced each other head-on. I don't think he had much ammunition left as I saw only small bursts of incendiaries pass me. I held my fire to a very short distance and just managed to clear him. Turning back, I saw him going down vertically.'

Dyson resumed his homeward flight, but three more Fiats apparently got onto his tail and his aircraft was damaged badly enough for him to crash-land. His six claims were at first treated with some scepticism, but Army units, which had witnessed the whole fight, provided adequate confirmation. Unseen by Dyson, one of the falling CR.42s had crashed into a Ba.65, bringing it down too. His total of seven confirmed kills in a single sortie set an unbroken record for the RAF.

Dyson had in fact jumped a formation of nine CR.42s from 368^{a} *Squadriglia*, escorting four Ba.65s of 16° *Gruppo*. He initially shot down the machine of Sergente Eugenio Cicognani, who bailed out. Diving away, Dyson had been followed by Tenente Amedeo Guidi, who decided to avenge the loss of his comrade. Thanks to his superior speed, the RAF pilot soon outdistanced his pursuer. Then Dyson met Capitano Bruno Locatelli and Sergente Maggiore Davide Colauzzi. They were at low altitude, having set three trucks alight in a strafing run. The 368^{a} *Squadriglia* diary presents a different account of what happened next;

'While still at low altitude, Capitano Locatelli and Sergente Maggiore Colauzzi were attacked by a Hurricane. After a short combat, which also involved Tenente Guidi of 368^{a} *Squadriglia*, the Hurricane caught fire.'

16° *Gruppo* had in fact lost the Ba.65 piloted by Maresciallo Antonio Gallerani, partly confirming Dyson's account. An additional loss had been suffered that morning when Tenente Vittorio Gnudi of 94^{a} *Squadriglia*, 8° *Gruppo* had been killed by Hurricanes of No 33 Sqn.

On the 12th, Capitano Guglielmo Arrabito of 82^{a} *Squadriglia* shot down a Blenheim I of No 45 Sqn near Sollum, while the Gladiators of No 3 Sqn RAAF claimed the CR.42 of 84^{a} *Squadriglia*, 10° *Gruppo* pilot Sergente Onorino Crestani. That day also saw 8° *Gruppo* removed from the frontline due to a paucity of serviceable aircraft. The remaining CR.42 units also reported a decline in combat efficiency, as they were now down to almost 50 per cent of their initial operational strength.

In East Africa, 412^{a} *Squadriglia* enjoyed yet more success on 12 December when it carried out an effective strafing attack on the advanced strip at Gaz Regeb. Five CR.42s destroyed four Hardys on the ground, although they mistakenly claimed them as five Vincents. Unit CO

Tenente Mario Visintini (front) poses for the photographer with Capitano Antonio Raffi at Gura on 12 December 1940. Earlier that day, during a strafing attack, Raffi's *Falco* had been hit by groundfire and he had been obliged to force-land behind enemy lines. Immediately, Visintini landed alongside his CO and took him aboard. Sat on Raffi's lap, he then took off again, set fire to the damaged Fiat and returned to base. This act was widely publicised in the Italian press (*Nicola Malizia*)

Capitano Raffi suffered an engine failure in his fighter after it was hit by ground fire, forcing him down behind Allied lines. Tenente Visintini landed, dispensed with his parachute and had Raffi climb into the fighter's snug cockpit. The ace duly flew the CR.42 back to Asmara sat on his CO's knees – but not before the abandoned *Falco* had been set on fire.

The weather improved in North Africa on the 13th, and this brought an increase in activity for V^{a} *Squadra.* At 0900 hrs, six Gladiators of No 3 Sqn RAAF, which had just intercepted a formation of five SM.79s from 33° *Gruppo,* were bounced by ten CR.42s of 9° *Gruppo,* led by Capitano Antonio Larsimont-Pergameni. In one of their last combats of the campaign, the pilots of 4° *Stormo* were finally able to avenge the losses inflicted by the Gladiators since August. They reported shooting down five of the RAAF biplanes, piloted by Flt Lt Gaden, who was killed, and Flg Offs Winten, Boyd, Gatward and Arthur.

Larsimont-Pergameni, an experienced pilot who had learned that opening fire from the closest possible range was not only the best way of conserving ammunition, but also of ensuring victory, was seen to collide with the Gladiator he was chasing. The latter lost its wings in the collision, while Larsimont-Pergameni, whose fuselage and rudder were badly damaged, made an emergency landing on Menastir airfield. Unfortunately for him, the airstrip had already been evacuated by the Italians due to the close proximity of British infantry. Larsimont-Pergameni had to abandon his damaged aircraft, which became a total loss. His victim was future ace Flg Off 'Woof' Arthur, who later recalled;

'I was chasing some Italian bombers when I suddenly realised that I was being attacked by an Italian fighter. Almost immediately, a shell went into my top mainplane, which tore it straight away and swung it back towards the tail. The bottom mainplane sort of followed it, but a bit behind. I had no control at all – just a completely loose control column – so I got out quickly '

Antonio Larsimont-Pergameni was born in Villa D'almè, near Bergamo, on 30 May 1912. In the pre-war years he had been a close friend of Giorgio Graffer, with whom he had shared his time at the *Accademia Aeronautica.* Like Graffer, he too was a skilled mountaineer, making many climbs. Larsimont-Pergameni had also fought in the Spanish Civil War, being among the first Italian pilots to fly operations in the autumn of 1936. Promoted to *squadriglia* CO in *XXIII Gruppo Asso di Bastoni,* he had been credited with four individual victories whilst flying the CR.32. Larsimont-Pergameni had also earned a reputation for being a good leader and a tough fighter.

His victory over Arthur represented his first individual claim of World War 2, and it made him an ace. Larsimont-Pergameni had also shared in the downing of No 55 Sqn Blenheim I L8394 on 27 September.

Tenente Visintini is seen with fellow 412ª *Squadriglia* pilots in front of a suitably marked CR.42 at Barentu, in Eritrea, in late 1940. They are, from left to right, Tenenti Cacciavillani and Visintini, Sottotenente D'Addetta, Tenente Di Pauli, Capitano Raffi and Sottotenente Levi. The *Squadriglia* emblem featured a red prancing horse superimposed onto a map of Africa, this motif bearing a strong resemblence to the 4° *Stormo* icon – many 412ª *Squadriglia* pilots had previously served with this unit (*via Giorgio Apostolo*)

Eventually succeeding Maggiore Botto as CO of 9° *Gruppo*, Larsimont-Pergameni continued to lead from the air until his unit was withdrawn from North Africa. He would later add two more victories to his tally while flying the C.202 over Malta, before being killed during a bombing raid on Sidi el-Barrani on 26 June 1942. Sadly missed, Larsimont-Pergameni was granted a posthumous *Medaglia d'oro al valor militare*, which was added to the five *Medaglie d'argento al valor militare* he had already won.

Two Hurricanes from No 274 Sqn were also downed by CR.42s on 13 December, although pilots from 9°, 13° and 151° *Gruppi* claimed only probable victories and aircraft damaged. In return, Flg Off Lapsley claimed a CR.42 destroyed, and No 33 Sqn was credited with three kills.

It was at this point, with the Italian fighter force depleted by the losses suffered in the previous month and Fiat unable to supply enough new machines, that Generale Francesco Pricolo, commander in chief of the *Regia Aeronautica*, published a memorandum on the employment of the fighter force. It stated that the pilots' aggression in seeking combat at every opportunity, even when badly outnumbered, was leading to too many losses. Pricolo's memorandum also pointed out that the losses were sometimes not proportional to those inflicted on the enemy. Moreover, they could not be made good by the factories or by the training schools.

Instead, it was decreed that pilots should accept combat, or attack, only when flying direct or indirect escort missions, or when intercepting enemy bombers. During fighter sweeps they should fight 'only under conditions of clear numerical superiority', and ground strafing was to be limited to special situations. With these instructions, Pricolo hoped that his pilots would continue to achieve successes, while reducing the present rate of loss, which when added to other causes was unsustainable.

14 December was a day of clear weather. Vª *Squadra Aerea*, answering the desperate call for help from an army now in full retreat, put up a maximum effort with all available aircraft. The *gruppi* of 4° *Stormo* were mainly deployed on strafing missions, while the CR.42s of 13° and 151° *Stormi*, or at least those machines still serviceable after five days of continuous operations in awful weather conditions and hasty retreats to new bases, tried to keep a protective umbrella over the subsequent waves of SM.79s attacking the advancing British troops.

Eleven *Falcos* of 151° *Gruppo* met a mixed formation of nine Blenheim Is from Nos 55 and 11 Sqns over Bardia. They shot down three or possibly four and severely damaged the others in what was probably the most successful interception of the campaign. Locatelli and Chiarini were flying in the Italian formation.

During the afternoon of the 14th, five CR.42s of 13° *Gruppo* were jumped by Hurricanes of No 274 Sqn while flying a standing patrol over Sidi Azeiz, where wave after wave of SM.79s were attacking the advanced elements of the 7th Armoured Division. The Fiats, led by the *Gruppo* CO, Tenente Colonello Revetria, were able to turn the tables on their opponents and shoot down the Hurricane of Sqn Ldr 'Paddy' Dunn – he force-landed for the second day running. Although the Italian unit suffered no losses, five victories were credited to No 274 Sqn.

While the CR.42s of 13° *Gruppo* were keeping the Hurricanes busy, the *Falco* pilots of 9° and 10° *Gruppi* flew endless strafing missions against the advancing British mechanised columns. And they found themselves flying virtually unopposed, as the RAF had been unable to get No 73 Sqn into the frontline, No 3 Sqn RAAF was all but grounded after the previous day's beating and No 112 Sqn had not a single airworthy Gladiator. The remaining two Hurricane squadrons (Nos 33 and 274) were depleted by losses and badly overstretched.

On the ground, the crack 11th Hussars had suffered particularly heavy losses in the vanguard of the advance. At the end of the day they had to be relieved, expressing admiration for their enemies. The troops reported that 'the handling of the CR.42s, despite very heavy AA fire, was impressive'. The day had ended with a clear tactical victory for the *Regia Aeronautica*. The advance of the Western Desert Force more than compensated for this, however, and all Italian fighter units had to vacate the big airfields in the Tobruk area. At Gambut and El Adem, many aircraft were awaiting repair or servicing, and these were lost to the Allies too. Added to the casualties already sustained during the previous days, as well as wear and tear suffered on the British side, there was an overall slackening of aerial activity in North Africa through to year-end.

Nevertheless, the 15th saw combat between Hurricanes of Nos 33 and 274 Sqns and CR.42s from 13° *Gruppo*, which were able to claim a single RAF fighter destroyed from both units. No 274 Sqn ace Flg Off Peter Wykeham-Barnes was credited with a CR.42 downed in return.

In East Africa, 412ª *Squadriglia* was in action on the night of 15/16 December when Wellesley L2690 of No 223 Sqn was intercepted and shot up. The aircraft was damaged beyond repair when it crash-landed back at its Wadi Gazouza base. This victory was probably another credited to Visintini, who wrote home, 'I climbed twice in the moonlight against enemy aeroplanes and took part in two combats. The enemy certainly had a bad time, and I hit one aeroplane fatally'. Some sources say this victory was scored on the night of 12/13 December, but Visintini is the only Italian pilot known to have claimed a nocturnal victory during this period.

The Hurricanes of No 274 Sqn, accompanied by others from No 73 Sqn, again took a toll of Italian bombers over Bardia, on the Libyan coast, on 16 December when they savaged an unescorted formation of SM.79s from 9°

Three CR.42s from 90ª *Squadriglia,* 10° *Gruppo* escort SM.79s from 15° *Stormo* during an attack on Sollum harbour on 28 December 1940. *Falcos* from both 10° and 23° *Gruppi* encountered Hurricanes during the course of the mission, and they counterattacked so vigorously that the RAF fighters 'were obliged to flee', according to an Italian combat account. Two Hurricanes were claimed as probably shot down by the pilots of 90ª and 91ª *Squadriglie.* The fighters were led by Maggiore Carlo Romagnoli, who flew with CR.42 ace Sergente Maggiore Leonardo Ferrulli as his wingman. It is possible that the aircraft depicted here are theirs – the one with the radio (the CR.42 closest to the camera boasts an aerial cable) could be Romagnoli's, as 10° *Gruppo* had just received a few radio-equipped machines. This particular SM.79 is from 54ª *Squadriglia,* 47° *Gruppo.* In a curious twist of fate, this *Gruppo* returned to Italy and was re-equipped with CR.42 fighter-bombers in May 1942. It was then posted back to North Africa, where the unit took part in the Battle of El Alamein (*Foto Pilon via Gabriele Brancaccio*)

Stormo. The RAF pilots had claimed six bombers destroyed by the time the CR.42s of 10° *Gruppo* arrived somewhat belatedly on the scene. The latter was able to claim only one probable victory over the Hurricane flown by Plt Off McFadden, who had to make a force-landing after being been chased 'up-country' by two CR.42s. Although his demise was attributed to the whole formation, it was possibly a victory for Franco Lucchini. The Hurricane units also claimed two *Falcos* destroyed.

The 17th saw two CR.42s of 13° *Gruppo* (flown by Sottotenentes Dario Magnabosco and Natale Cima) shot down by Hurricanes of No 33 Sqn, while N2627, flown by No 274 Sqn's Plt Off Strong, force-landed, having possibly been hit by the combined fire of future ace Tenente Reiner and another pilot.

Operations resumed over Greece on the 18th, when a Blenheim IF of No 30 Sqn was shot down during a raid on Valona harbour. Three RAF aircraft had been intercepted by six CR.42s of 150° *Gruppo*, led by Tenente Ugo Drago – three G.50bis from 154° *Gruppo* were also involved. The Italians claimed three probables. Shortly before midday 13 Gladiators of No 80 Sqn took on five SM.79s and their fighter escorts over Tepelene. Two were downed by the bombers' defensive fire and AA, but none fell to the *Falcos*.

Hurricanes from Nos 33 and 274 Sqns again 'mixed it' with SM.79s and escorting CR.42s over the Sollum-Gambut area of Libya on 19 December, and six *Falcos* were claimed by the RAF pilots. The Italians admitted that ace Sergente Maggiore Leonardo Ferrulli of 91ª *Squadriglia*, 10° *Gruppo* was shot down on the 19th (he survived unscathed) and claimed four Hurricanes in return. By then 9° and 13° *Gruppi* had retreated to Italy, their place in Libya being taken by 20 CR.42s of 23° *Gruppo* that had flown in from the Italian mainland on the 16th. Operations continued at a much reduced pace, with daily missions being flown to escort SM.79s with strong formations of fighters.

On the morning of the 21st, another battle for air superiority took place in Greek skies close to Argyrokastron when 15 CR.42s of 160° *Gruppo*, led by Maggiore Molinari, and six *Falcos* of 150° *Gruppo*, led by Capitano Luigi Corsini, intercepted ten Gladiators of No 80 Sqn that were attacking Z.1007bis. A fierce 25-minute dogfight ensued, at the end of which three CR.42s failed to return, together with two Gladiators.

The opposing COs were among those lost, Sqn Ldr Hickey perishing when his parachute caught fire as he bailed out of his blazing Gladiator. Maggiore Molinari was more fortunate, for after claiming to have shot down two fighters, he was obliged to force-land his damaged machine in a dry river bed. Tenente Edoardo Crainz of 394ª *Squadriglia* had in fact saved Molinari's life by shooting down a Gladiator that was on his tail attempting to finish him off. Crainz had also claimed an additional victory, while Tenente Eber Giudice was credited with two more and Capitano Arcangeletti one. Three victories were also claimed as shared, and two were awarded to 150° *Gruppo*. Despite these successes, two more outstanding pilots had been killed – Tenentes Carancini and Frascadore.

The Gladiator pilots had indeed suffered their worst losses since the start of the campaign, with Hickey and Flg Off A D Ripley being killed. Sgt Gregory's engine and undercarriage had also been damaged by a series of frontal attacks from a CR.42 that left him wounded in the right eye

CR.42 '394-7' of Tenente Edoardo Crainz of 394ª *Squadriglia*, 160° *Gruppo* is seen here after it had been patched up following combat with No 80 Sqn Gladiators on 21 December 1940. Crainz claimed two British fighters destroyed, but No 80 Sqn was in turn credited with downing eight Italian aircraft for the loss of two Gladiators. 150° and 160° *Gruppi* had also claimed eight enemy aircraft destroyed and three probables, while losing two aircraft and one force-landed. Crainz claimed his third, and last victory, over a Greek Gladiator on 9 February (*Nicola Malizia*)

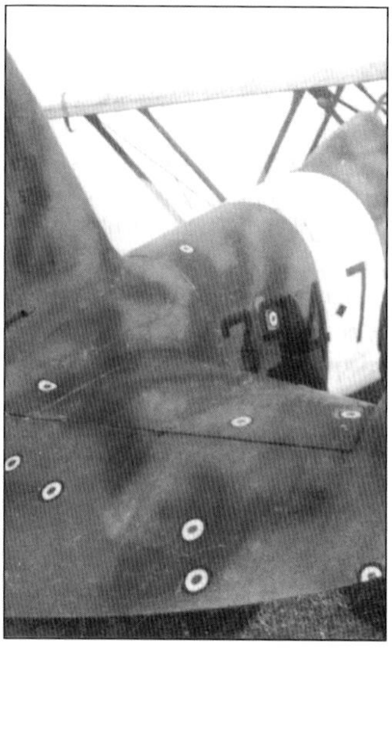

and barely able to save himself from a 'desperate position'. Plt Off Bill Vale returned in an aircraft riddled by explosive bullets, while Flg Off Linnard was hit in the left leg.

Flt Lt Pattle noted that 'the enemy fighters employed a definite plan of attack. Attacking from superior height, they maintained that height by attacking the Gladiators singly and in quick succession, and climbing after each attack. The Gladiators, forced to evade, were unable to climb. For fully five minutes I was kept on the defensive, without being able to fire a shot in return'. Nevertheless, No 80 Sqn claimed eight confirmed kills and three probables.

A somewhat war-weary Capitano Paolo Arcangeletti poses for the photographer. Arriving from 21° *Gruppo* on November 1940, this 28-year-old permanent officer was to remain in the ranks of 160° *Gruppo* for the duration of the war, claiming one and three shared victories during the Greek campaign. Arcangeletti had previously claimed three victories in Spain, and would eventually finish the war as an ace with five victories to his name (*Fulvio Chianese – Associazione Culturale 4° Stormo di Gorizia*)

This fight brought an end to operations by No 80 Sqn in Greece. Four pilots killed (including the CO) and three wounded in just a month of operations had left the unit badly undermanned. Replaced by 21 *Mira* of *EVA* and sent back to the Athens area, No 80 Sqn would not see further action over the frontline until the end of January. The *Regia Aeronautica* had finally gained air superiority, but at the cost of 12 fighters – three for each Gladiator shot down.

CR.42s and Hurricanes clashed over Libya once again on 23 December, resulting in No 274 Sqn losing P5176, flown by Flg Off Greenhill, to 10° *Gruppo's* fighters. The Italians claimed two kills and the British a CR.42. On Boxing Day, No 3 Sqn RAAF returned to the action in its Gladiators when it took on five SM.79s and as many as 24 CR.42 escorts over Bardia. The unit claimed two *Falcos* and a probable for no loss, while the Italians were credited with three Gladiators destroyed. The only loss suffered by either side befell 74ª *Squadriglia*, which had its CO, Capitano Guido Bobba, killed. No 33 Sqn claimed two CR.42s the following day and the Italians three fighters (again, there were no losses), with by a single *Falco* victory reported on the 28th.

In Greece, December ended with three more Blenheims being shot down by CR.42s. A machine from No 211 Sqn was lost on the 26th, a Greek bomber of 32 *Mira* on the 30th and another machine from No 211 Sqn on the 31st. They were all claimed by 150° *Gruppo* pilots.

There was yet another victory for the Gladiators of No 1 Sqn SAAF in East Africa on 27 December. In a dogfight over Gedaref, three Gladiators were able to corner the CR.42 of Sottotenente Filippo Sola of the East Africa air force HQ who was attached to 412ª *Squadriglia*. He was killed. The last combat of the year in this region took place two days later when Tenente Franco De Micheli and Sottotenente Osvaldo Bartolozzi of 413ª *Squadriglia* scrambled to intercept four Hurricanes of No 2 Sqn SAAF that were raiding Bardera. They were able to shoot down Lt J A Kok and Flt Lt R S Blake, who was then the SAAF's top-scoring pilot in East

Leonardo Ferrulli of 91ª *Squadriglia* was one of the most successful Italian aces. Born in Brindisi on 1 January 1918, he participated in the Spanish Civil War (despite being only 20) and was credited with one individual victory. Once back in Italy, Ferrulli enlisted in the elite 91ª *Squadriglia* of 10° *Gruppo,* where he remained for the rest of the war. His individual achievements during the first North African campaign have been reconstructed during post-war studies because the official documents credit him with only shared victories. Ferrulli was reputed to have shot down five Commonwealth aircraft while flying the CR.42, thus making him one of the relatively few known aces on the type. Having claimed 21 and three shared victories, Ferrulli was killed in combat over Sicily on 5 July 1943 *(Fulvio Chianese – Associazione Culturale 4° Stormo di Gorizia)*

Africa with three victories to his credit. Bartolozzi, who downed Blake, had only been flying the CR.42 for about a week!

So ended 1940, and with it a period of six-and-a-half months of hard fighting for the CR.42s. This had been characterised by increasingly intense actions during which the *Falco gruppi* had been able to shoot down at least 150 enemy aircraft for the loss of around 75 of their own in aerial combat.

Since the beginning of the campaigns in North and East Africa, the Fiats had demonstrated their superiority over the Blenheims and Wellesleys that formed the backbone of the Commonwealth bomber force in the two African fronts. Indeed, they had accounted for a considerable number of both types.

On the other hand, the CR.42 pilots had been particularly surprised by the more manoeuvrable Gladiators, suffering heavy losses while trying to dogfight with them. These losses were reduced by the adoption of better tactics that exploited the *Falco's* superior diving speed. Until that point the victory-loss ratio had favoured pilots of the Gloster biplane. However, in bad weather conditions the radio-equipped Gladiator with its enclosed cockpit continued to retain a definite advantage over the Fiat fighter.

The appearance of the Hurricane, limited in numbers by the demands of Fighter Command's UK-based squadrons and hampered in performance by the cumbersome Vokes sand filters required for operations in Africa, did not initially have a major impact on the Fiat units. But from December onwards, the arrival of the fighter in larger numbers, their avoidance of dogfights with the Italian biplanes, coupled with decreasing numbers of serviceable *Falcos*, caused Italian losses to steadily rise. The CR.42 had to be replaced as the *Regia Aeronautica's* main frontline fighter by faster monoplanes.

Of the 11 *gruppi* totally or partially equipped with the CR.42 at the beginning of the war, one – 157° – had been virtually withdrawn to second-line duties by the end of 1940. Its fighters were used to make good the losses suffered by the other *gruppi*. Another – 17° – had to convert back to the C.200, three more – 8°, 9° and 13° – had just been withdrawn to Italy, where they too would receive C.200s, and 10° *Gruppo* would soon follow. Only 160° *Gruppo* and the *gruppi* previously part of 3° and 53° *Stormi* were to remain equipped with the *Falco* well into 1941. But from the spring they would increasingly be employed on second-line duties as point defenders or convoy escorts. Only two units had re-equipped with the *Falco* in the meantime – 3° *Gruppo* and, later, 161° *Gruppo*. But they were to see only limited action in secondary sectors like Sardinia and Rhodes.

At the beginning of 1941, however, six CR.42 *gruppi* remained in the frontline, together with the *squadriglie Autonome* in East Africa. They opposed Commonwealth squadrons now almost totally equipped with Hurricanes as best they could. A period of grievous losses was about to begin.

A damaged and engineless CR.42 of 82ª *Squadriglia* lies abandoned on a desert airfield in eastern Libya in December 1940 (*Marco Gargari*)

COLOUR PLATES

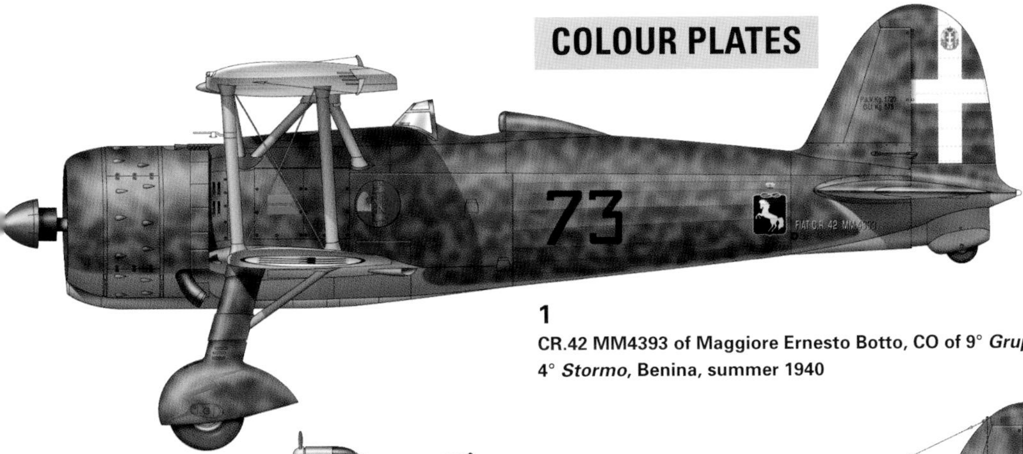

1
CR.42 MM4393 of Maggiore Ernesto Botto, CO of 9° *Gruppo*, 4° *Stormo*, Benina, summer 1940

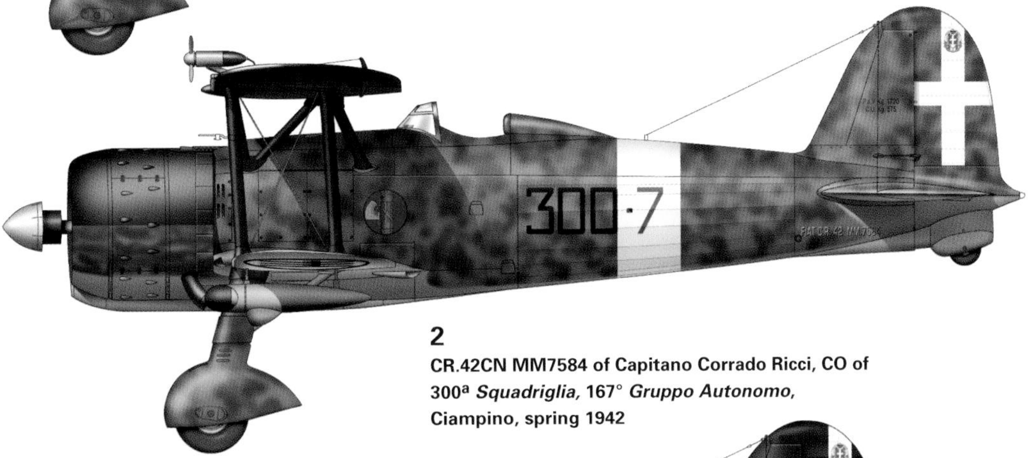

2
CR.42CN MM7584 of Capitano Corrado Ricci, CO of 300ª *Squadriglia*, 167° *Gruppo Autonomo*, Ciampino, spring 1942

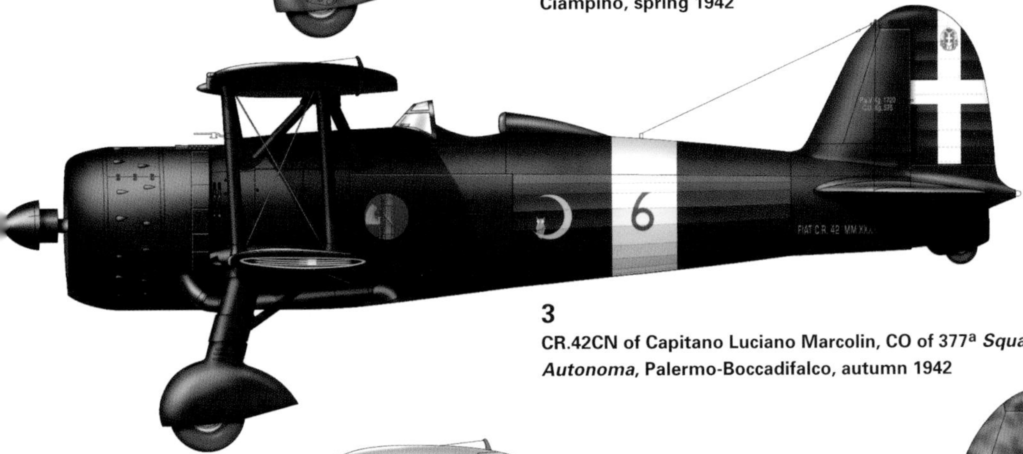

3
CR.42CN of Capitano Luciano Marcolin, CO of 377ª *Squadriglia Autonoma*, Palermo-Boccadifalco, autumn 1942

4
CR.42 of 77ª *Squadriglia*, 13° *Gruppo*, 2° *Stormo*, Castelbenito, summer 1940

5

CR.42 MM5649 of 96ª *Squadriglia*, 9° *Gruppo*, 4° *Stormo*, El Adem, autumn 1940

6

CR.42 (serial unknown) of Sergente Maggiore Sante Morandi, 413ª *Squadriglia Autonoma*, Somaliland, August 1940

7

CR.42 MM5701 of Sergente Pietro Salvadori, 95ª *Squadriglia*, 18° *Gruppo*, 56° *Stormo*, Ursel, 11 November 1940

8

CR.42 MM4387 of 77ª *Squadriglia*, 13° *Gruppo*, 2° *Stormo*, Castelbenito, summer 1940

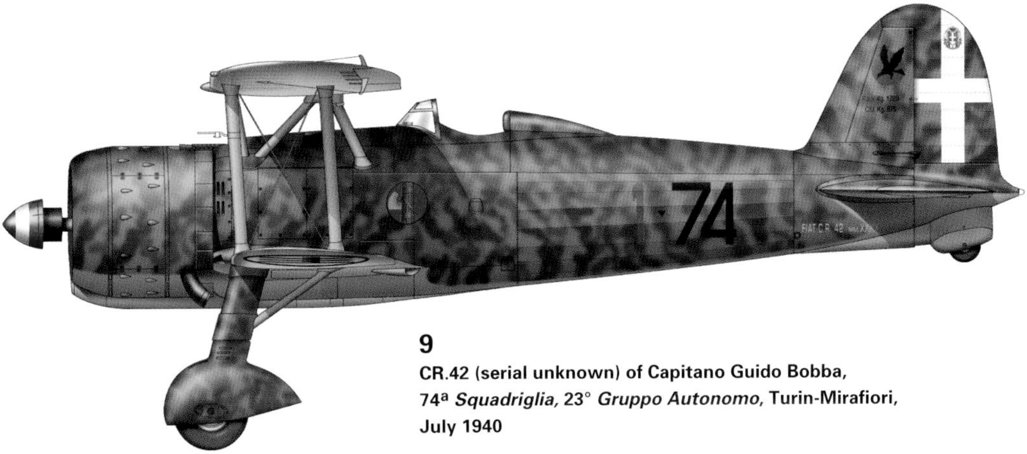

9

CR.42 (serial unknown) of Capitano Guido Bobba, 74a *Squadriglia*, 23° *Gruppo Autonomo*, Turin-Mirafiori, July 1940

10

CR.42 (serial unknown) of Sottotenente Franco Bordoni-Bisleri, 95a *Squadriglia*, 18° *Gruppo*, 3° *Stormo*, Mirafiori, summer 1940

11

CR.42 (serial unknown) of Tenente Edoardo Crainz, 394a *Squadriglia*, 160° *Gruppo Autonomo*, Koritza, December 1940

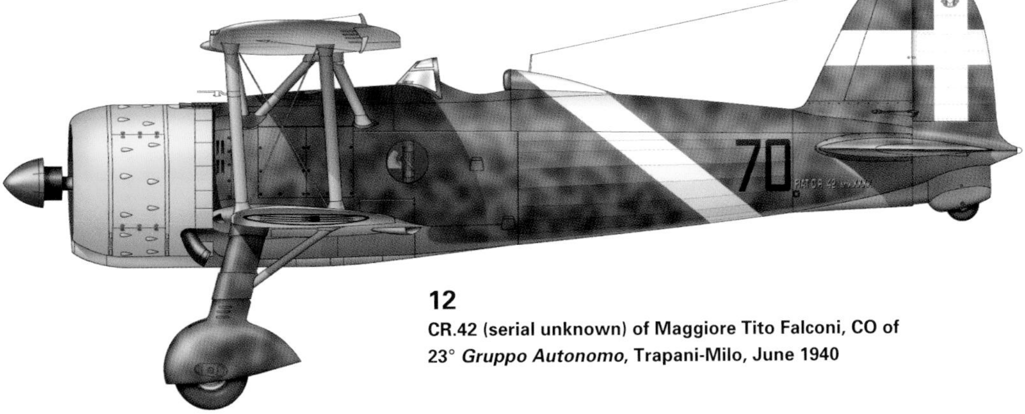

12

CR.42 (serial unknown) of Maggiore Tito Falconi, CO of 23° *Gruppo Autonomo*, Trapani-Milo, June 1940

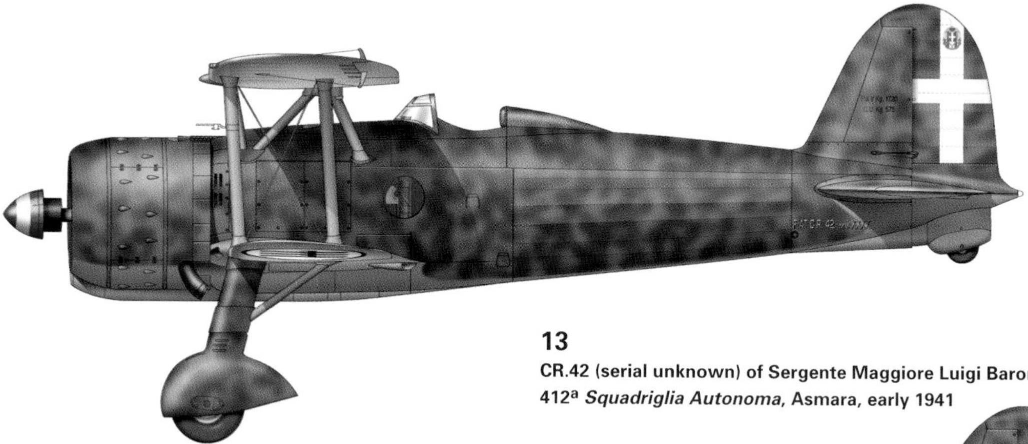

13

CR.42 (serial unknown) of Sergente Maggiore Luigi Baron, 412ª *Squadriglia Autonoma*, Asmara, early 1941

14

CR.42 (serial unknown) of Tenente Mario Visintini, 412ª *Squadriglia Autonoma*, Barentu, late 1940

15

CR.42 MM4382 of Tenente Mario Rigatti, 75ª *Squadriglia*, 23° *Gruppo Autonomo*, Comiso, August 1940

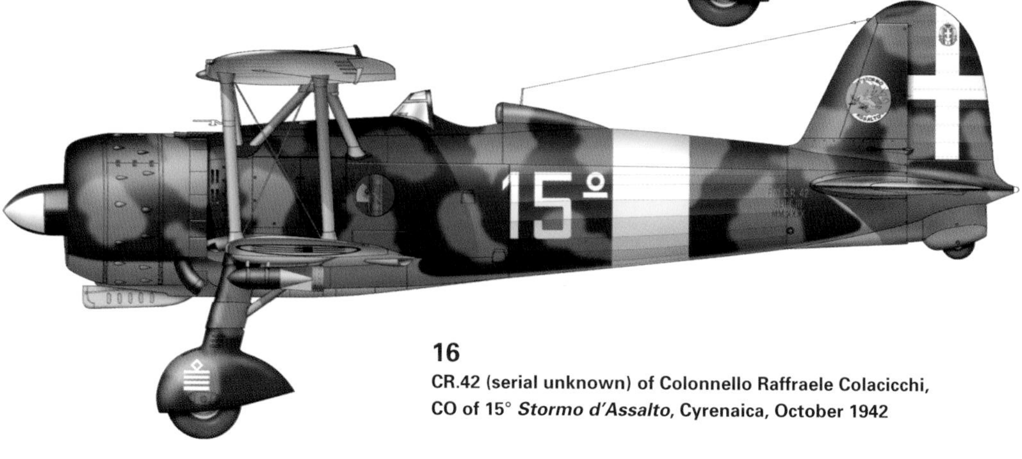

16

CR.42 (serial unknown) of Colonnello Raffraele Colacicchi, CO of 15° *Stormo d'Assalto*, Cyrenaica, October 1942

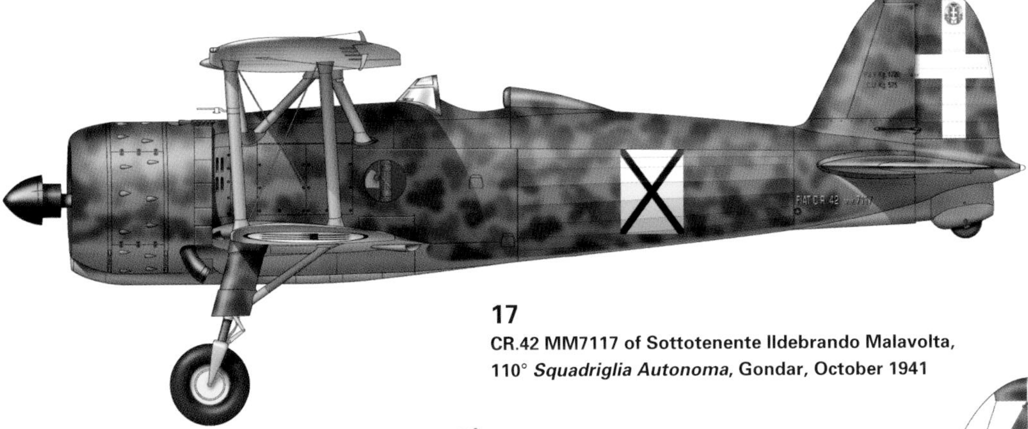

17

CR.42 MM7117 of Sottotenente Ildebrando Malavolta, 110° *Squadriglia Autonoma*, Gondar, October 1941

18

CR.42 (serial unknown) of Colonello Arrigo Tessari, CO of 53° *Stormo*, Turin, 10 October 1940

19

CR.42 (serial unknown) of Capitano Giorgio Graffer, 365ª *Squadriglia*, 150° *Gruppo Autonomo*, Argyrokastron, November 1940

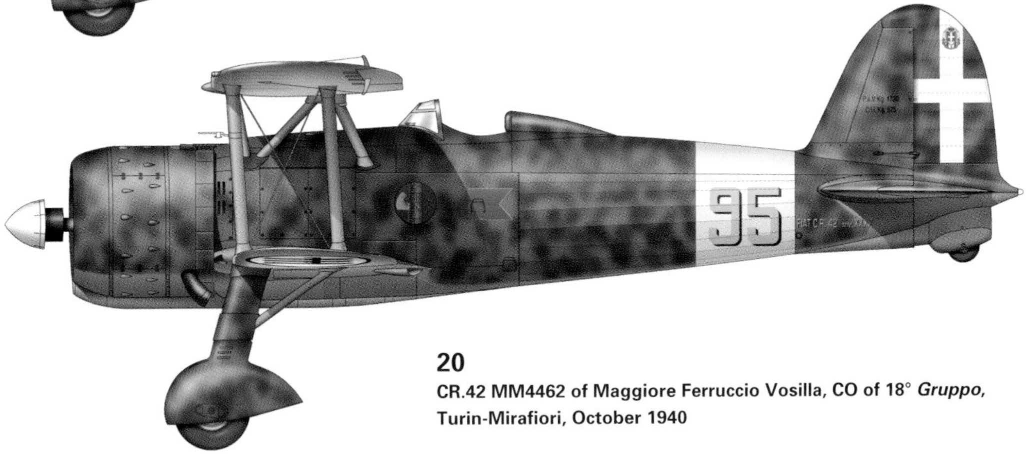

20

CR.42 MM4462 of Maggiore Ferruccio Vosilla, CO of 18° *Gruppo*, Turin-Mirafiori, October 1940

21

CR.42 (serial unknown) of Sergente Luigi Gorrini, 85ª *Squadriglia,* 18° *Gruppo,* 3° *Stormo*, Villanova D'Albenga, June 1940

22

CR.42 MM4304 of Capitano Corrado Santoro, 413ª *Squadriglia Autonoma,* Diredawa, August 1940

23

CR.42 MM4308 of Tenente Enzo Martissa, 91ª *Squadriglia,* 10° *Gruppo,* 4° *Stormo*, El Adem, August 1940

24

CR.42 of Tenente Colonello Rolando Pratelli, CO of 150° *Gruppo,* Valona, March 1941

25
CR.42 MM5024 of Capitano Aldo Li Greci, CO of 385ª *Squadriglia,* 157° *Gruppo,* 1° *Stormo,* Trapani-Milo, July 1940

26
CR.42 (serial unknown) of Capitano Virginio Teucci, CO of 375ª *Squadriglia,* 160° *Gruppo,* Brindisi, June 1941

27
CR.42 (serial unknown) of 368ª *Squadriglia,* 151° *Gruppo,* Mellaha, April 1941

28
CR.42 R.5 of 4/II/1 *Aé,* Nivelles, May 1940

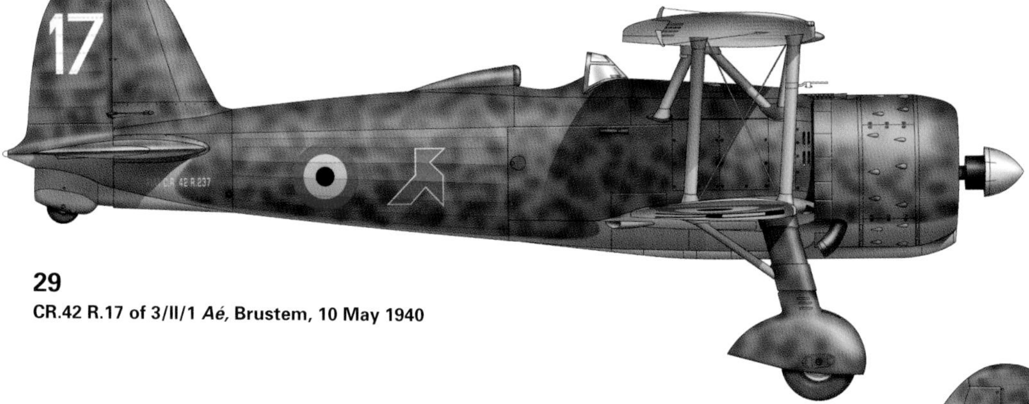

29

CR.42 R.17 of 3/II/1 *Aé*, Brustem, 10 May 1940

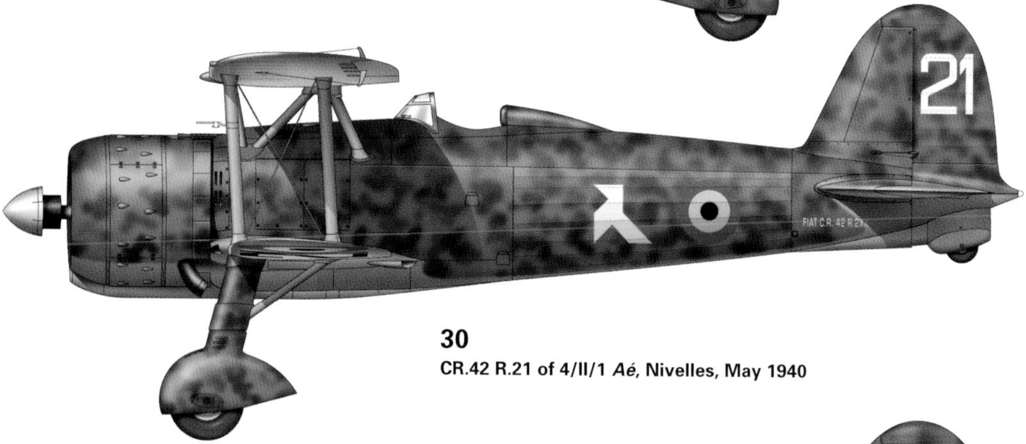

30

CR.42 R.21 of 4/II/1 *Aé*, Nivelles, May 1940

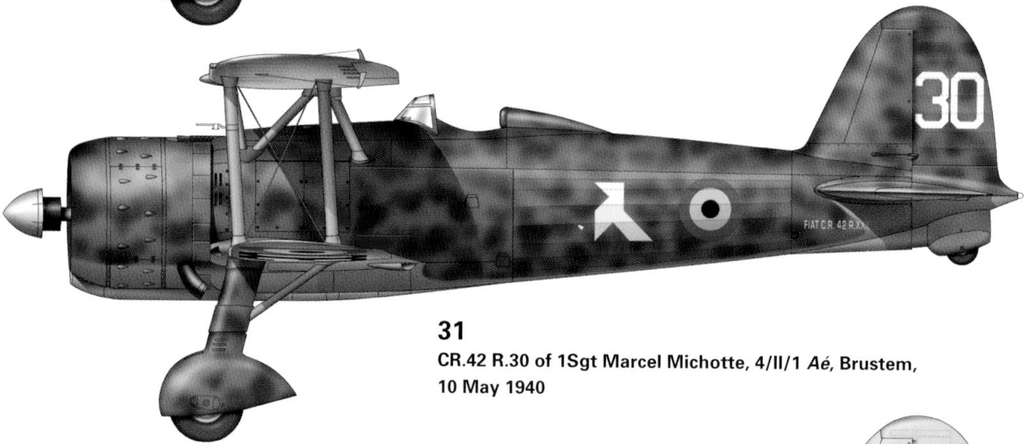

31

CR.42 R.30 of 1Sgt Marcel Michotte, 4/II/1 *Aé*, Brustem, 10 May 1940

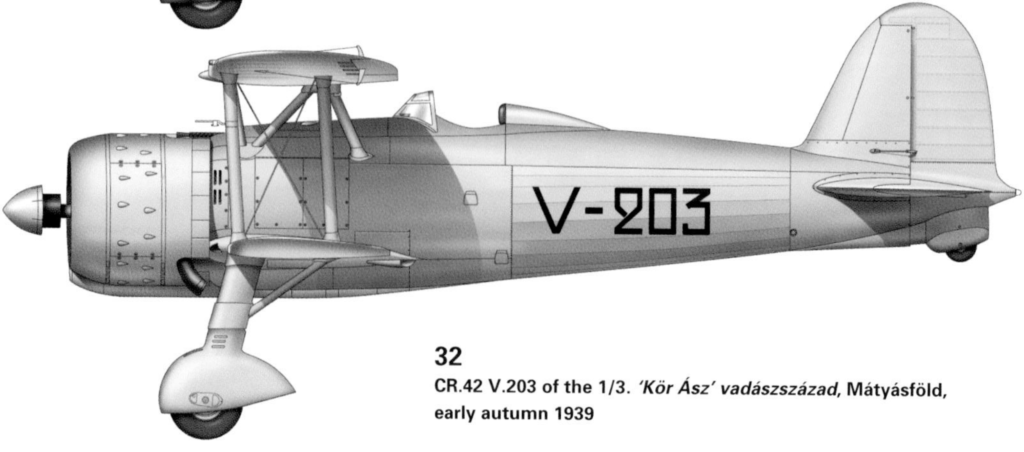

32

CR.42 V.203 of the 1/3. *'Kör Ász' vadászszázad*, Mátyásföld, early autumn 1939

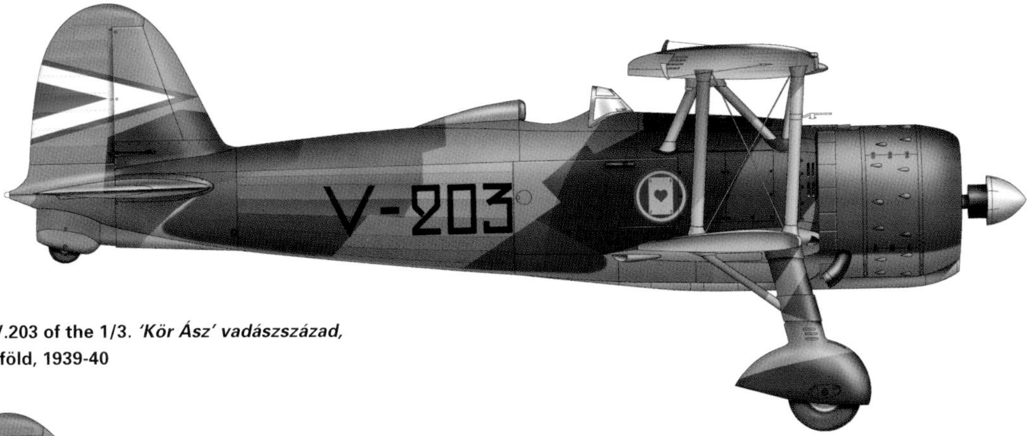

33

CR.42 V.203 of the 1/3. *'Kör Ász' vadászszázad,* Mátyásföld, 1939-40

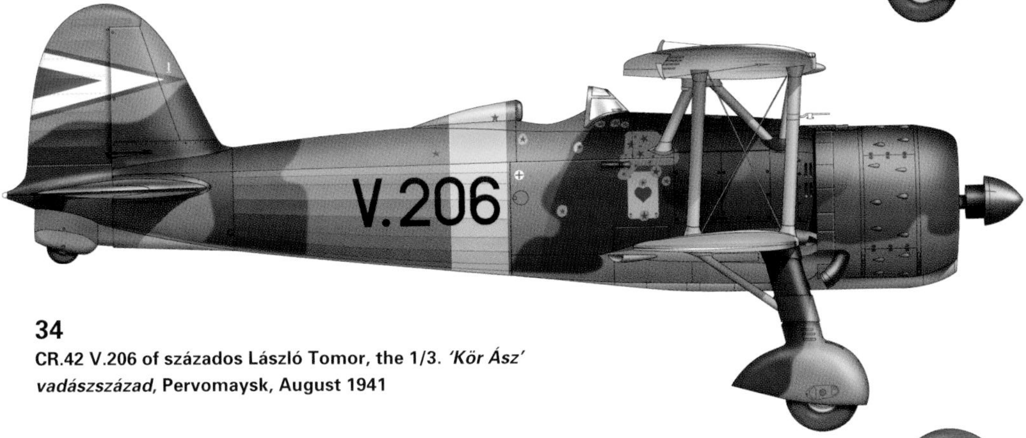

34

CR.42 V.206 of százados László Tomor, the 1/3. *'Kör Ász' vadászszázad,* Pervomaysk, August 1941

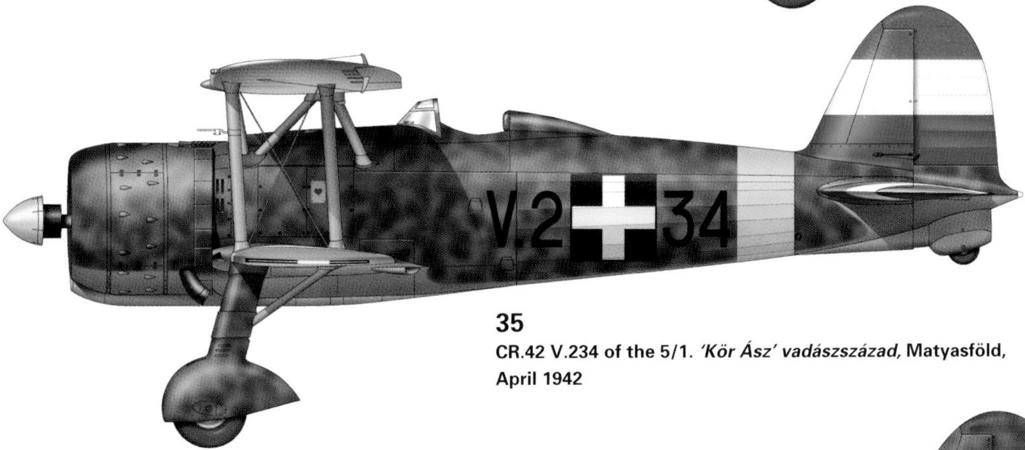

35

CR.42 V.234 of the 5/1. *'Kör Ász' vadászszázad,* Matyasföld, April 1942

36

CR.42 V.267 of föhadnagy László Kázár, the 2/3. *'Ricsi' vadászszázad,* Eastern Front, late summer 1941

37
CR.42LW (serial unknown) of Feldwebel Horst Greßler, 2./NSGr. 9, Viterbo, spring 1944

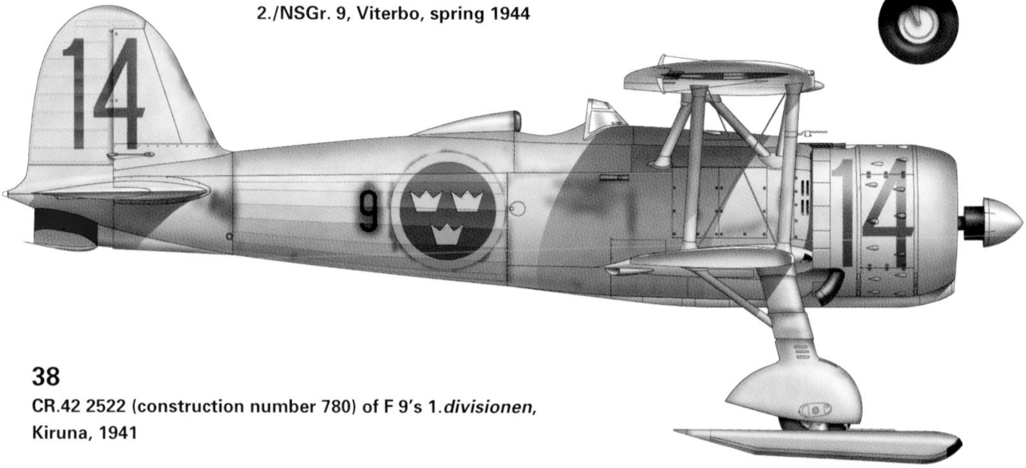

38
CR.42 2522 (construction number 780) of F 9's 1.*divisionen*, Kiruna, 1941

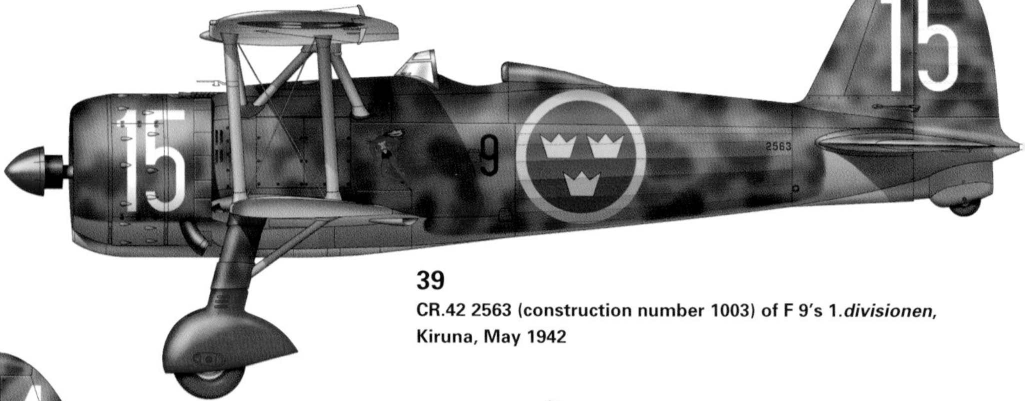

39
CR.42 2563 (construction number 1003) of F 9's 1.*divisionen*, Kiruna, May 1942

40
CR.42 (serial and construction number unknown) of F 9's 2.*divisionen*, Ånnsjön, February 1944

1941 – THE HARDEST YEAR

The first CR.42 combat of 1941 came on 3 January, when the 6th Australian Division began its offensive against the Italian stronghold of Bardia. Sergente Mario Veronesi of 84ª *Squadriglia* scrambled alone to intercept two Blenheim Is of No 45 Sqn over Gazala. He duly shot down L8479, which crashed with the loss of its crew. The second machine, flown by Flt Lt Paine, landed back at Quotafiyah so badly damaged as to be declared unserviceable. Paine reported that 'the enemy was a most persistent and first-class pilot'. In fact, Veronesi ended the war with 11 individual victories to his credit.

The following afternoon, six Hurricanes of No 274 Sqn were out singly or in pairs searching for Italian bombers. Flt Sgt Morris and Sgt Hulbert encountered an Italian formation escorted by a substantial number of CR.42s from 23° and 10° *Gruppi*. Morris reported that 'the escort was well spaced around the main force. The attack by CR.42s was very determined'. Moments later he was shot down, although he managed to make a force-landing. Hulbert was killed, however, probably by Tenente Pietro Calistri, temporary CO of 75ª *Squadriglia*.

Several hours earlier, 10° *Gruppo* had lost Tenente Ennio Grifoni, who was killed in an engagement with Hurricanes (one of which was flown by Morris). Another pilot known to have claimed an individual victory that day was Sergente Maggiore Leonardo Ferrulli of 91ª *Squadriglia*,

On 5 January 10° *Gruppo* was recalled to Italy, and operations by 23° *Gruppo*, whose remaining fighters had been badly mauled by Hurricanes of Nos 274 and 73 Sqns during the course of the day, came to a temporary end. The Hurricanes had shot down no fewer than five CR.42s without loss during an early afternoon engagement over Gambut. Among the four pilots killed was Sottotenente Oscar Abello, who had three victories to his name. He had been surprised on landing by ace Plt Off 'Imshi' Mason, while *Sottotenente* Leopoldo Marangoni had fallen victim to high-scoring No 274 Sqn CO Sqn Ldr 'Paddy' Dunn. Both pilots received posthumous *Medaglie d'oro al valor militare.*

They had been part of a 17-strong formation tasked with escorting SM.79s, and had desperately tried to protect their charges. The *Falcos* were continuously targeted by Hurricanes flown by high-scoring aces such as Mason, Dunn, Flt Sgt Alfred Marshall (of No 73 Sqn) and Flt Lt Peter Wykeham-Barnes, who made hit-and-run attacks on both the fighters and the bombers. One of the surviving pilots remembered;

'We were 17 in number, and we escorted five bombers ordered to attack enemy positions. The enemy reaction was very strong, and we had to withstand three consecutive battles. It was during the second attack, just after leaving the target area over the desert west of Bardia, that Leopoldo Marangoni was surprised by a Hurricane. So was his wingman.

Both left the formation. The attack was lightning-swift, and they were unable to avoid it. We were unable to help them, or to see what happened to them because we had to guard against further attacks.'

This combat represented a real turning point in the campaign. From now on the superiority of the British monoplanes became undisputed among the Italian fighter forces, which until then had fought them on equal terms. Moreover, with the retreat of 23° *Gruppo* to Derna, and with 151° *Gruppo's* aircraft undergoing desperately needed maintenance, no other *Falco* units remained operational over the frontline.

A CR.42 of 150° *Gruppo* taxies in after landing at an airfield near Valona. It is about to be swung round with the help of a burst of power and the mechanics holding onto the starboard wing (*Giorgio Apostolo*)

The situation was not so dire for the CR.42 in the Balkans, however, and on 6 January 150° *Gruppo* shot down a Blenheim I of No 211 Sqn over Valona – two more crash-landed and three were badly damaged. The Italian pilots claimed six destroyed, with three being credited to Sergente Osvaldo Bartolaccini. By now, the CR.42s were being replaced in the Balkans by the faster G.50s of 24° and 154° *Gruppi,* which had been scoring at the same rate as the *Falco* units, but with fewer losses.

9 January saw two more CR.42s destroyed by No 274 Sqn over Martuba, one falling to Plt Off Mason and the second to SAAF ace Lt Bob Talbot. Malta saw its first action of the new year on this date when C.200s strafed Luqa airfield and Ju 87s, escorted by ten CR.42s from 23° *Gruppo 'Nucleo'*, attacked Kalafrana. Two Macchis were downed by Hurricanes from No 261 Sqn, but the *Falcos* escaped unscathed.

On 19 January CR.42s again appeard over Malta when they escorted Ju 87s targeting the battle-damaged carrier HMS *Illustrious* in Grand Harbour. A single aircraft from 70ª *Squadriglia,* flown by Sergente Maggiore Iacone, was shot up by ace Flt Lt James Maclachlan, forcing the pilot to bail out north of Valetta. Maclachlan claimed four victories and a probable, with the CR.42 ironically being the probable! The following day 23° *Gruppo 'Nucleo'* became 156° *Gruppo Autonomo* (comprising 379ª and 380ª *Squadriglie*), led by ace Capitano Luigi Filippi.

A week earlier, on 12 January, 412ª *Squadriglia* had scored its first victories for 1941 when a Gladiator of No 1 Sqn SAAF was downed over Aroma and a Hardy of No 237 Sqn destroyed near Tessenei. A new Commonwealth offensive opened in the northern sector of the front on 20 January, and the CR.42s strafed the advancing troops. They enjoyed great success, with the 10th *Jhansi* Indian Infantry Brigade in particular being delayed in its

CR.42s from 375ª *Squadriglia,* 160° *Gruppo* sit lined up at Paramythia, in Greece in early 1941. The fighter nearest to the camera is '375-3' of Capitano Virginio Teucci (*Roberto Gentilli*)

advance and its commanding officer, Gen William Slim, wounded by strafing fire from a *Falco*. 412ª *Squadriglia* suffered three losses, however.

On the 21st the Australians launched their attack on Tobruk, and 151° *Gruppo* was rushed back into the frontline with 18 CR.42s. The Italian fortress fell quickly, and British troops reached the Benghazi region, where, on the 26th, five Hurricanes of No 274 Sqn intercepted seven CR.42s from 368ª *Squadriglia*, together with three G.50s of 2° *Gruppo*. Flg Off Mason single-handedly attacked the Italian formation, downing the Fiats of Maresciallo Guido Paparatti and Sottotenente Alfonso Nutti, both of whom were killed. Intent in gaining his last kill, Mason was in turn shot down by Sergente Maggiore Annibale Ricotti, who saw a Hurricane in front of him chasing another CR.42. He fired at it and saw the fighter going down, but at that same moment Ricotti spotted the *Falco* that the Hurricane had been chasing crash.

On the 29th 18° *Gruppo* arrived in Libya from Italy, having recovered from its adventures over England. However, its aircraft lacked sand-filters, as had those of *23° Gruppo* posted in the previous month. This meant that 18° *Gruppo* could not leave Tripoli. That same day, over the frontline, 23° *Gruppo* enjoyed a rare success when it downed the lone No 208 Sqn Hurricane of Flg Off L T Benson, killing the pilot. Only later was it realised that Benson had just delivered a message containing information about Sergente Cesare Sironi from 23° *Gruppo*, who had been missing since 24 January. The Hurricane had been attacked by Sergente Sanguettoli of 74ª *Squadriglia*. Italian fighters later flew over British troops and dropped a message of apology for this mistake, and to report that Benson had been buried with full military honours.

The following afternoon, as Australian troops seized Derna, Flg Offs 'Imshi' Mason and fellow ace Tom Patterson of No 274 Sqn flew over Benina airfield, near Benghazi, during a free sweep. Here, they spotted the CR.42 flown by Sergente Mario Turchi of 368ª *Squadriglia* on their starboard beam, 2000 ft below them. Although outnumbered, the young *sergente*, who had taken off to fly a standing patrol over Benina, fought tenaciously. Patterson's Hurricane was soon hit, forcing him to leave the battle with a shrapnel wound in his left arm. Turchi then started a series of head-on attacks on Mason, who recalled;

'This CR.42 pilot was very tough. We kept making head-on attacks, where we rushed at each other until we were at point-blank range. Then we shot past each other. Usually, my attacks were successful, but this fellow wouldn't go down. On the fourth attack we were rushing at each other, firing. This time he didn't pull out but came straight on. I pulled up instinctively and, as he passed beneath my wing, I felt a crash and a bump. I thought we had collided. I had a glimpse of him going straight on, burning. I now realised that I had been hit – we had not collided.'

Mason, who at the time was the leading RAF ace in the Mediterranean with 13 victories, was slightly wounded in the side. His aircraft had been badly shot up, although he was able to return to Gazala and land. Mason's first impression, that the aircraft had collided, had been right, for Turchi had lost the tip of this upper wing and suffered airscrew cuts in his lower wing. Mason abandoned the fight, leaving a trail of white smoke. His aircraft was claimed as damaged. The Italian pilot landed his Fiat, which was only slightly damaged, to a hero's welcome – Turchi's comrades had witnessed his successful combat from the airfield below.

One of those to see this engagement was squadronmate Tenente Zuffi, who noted, 'The enemies, despite their superior vertical and level speed, were always dominated, giving the impression of being easy prey if we were able to use our superior manoeuvrability'. Mario Turchi was awarded the *Medaglia d'argento al valor militare* for this combat.

The following day 368ª *Squadriglia* lost its CO, Capitano Bruno Locatelli. Just back from a short period of leave in Italy, he was hit by light ground fire during a reconnaissance mission. He bailed out with slight burns and was immediately taken prisoner.

There was plenty of action involving CR.42s in East Africa in late January, with 412ª *Squadriglia* finding itself in the thick of the fighting. The 29th saw a large dogfight fought over Gura between CR.42s and Gladiators of No 1 Sqn SAAF. The latter claimed five kills, although no *Falcos* were lost. Three had been badly shot up, however, including the fighters of Capitano Raffi and future ace Maresciallo Aroldo Soffritti.

Commonwealth troops that had invaded the Italian colony from Eritrea had had to halt their advance in early February under the slopes of the Keren mountain range. There, a long and bloody struggle would begin that lasted until late March. No 1 Sqn SAAF, reinforced with more Hurricanes, began a period of aggressive patrolling over Italian-held territory. Its pilots were always challenged by 412ª *Squadriglia*, despite the CR.42's increasing inferiority. The *Falco* still posed a threat to bomber and reconnaissance types, however, and on the 2nd Maresciallo Soffritti claimed his first kill when he downed a Lysander of No 237 Sqn.

Born in Bondeno on 5 April 1913, Soffritti had received his qualification as a pilot in October 1934. After serving in Libya and Gorizia with 4° *Stormo*, he resigned his commmission and headed to East Africa, where he had acquired some land with a farmer friend. Soffritti's life on the land was overtaken by the war, however, and he rejoined the air force, initially flying bombers, before transferring to 412ª *Squadriglia*. In January-February 1941, Soffritti often sortied up to four times a day over the Keren area, claiming seven victories to become the war's third-ranking CR.42 ace. With the defeat of the Italian Army in the sector, Soffritti was captured and eventually repatriated to Italy in 1946.

A Blenheim IV of No 55 Sqn provided 151° *Gruppo* with a confirmed kill over Libya on 2 February, a second bomber being forced to crash-land near Gazala. The unit had tangled with Hurricanes of No 73 Sqn the previous day, although no aircraft were lost by either side.

More fighting in East Africa on 3 February saw the loss of Maresciallo Enzo Omiccioli of 413ª *Squadriglia* and Sottotenente Vincenzo D'Addetta of 412ª *Squadriglia*. Omiccioli was actually serving with 410ª *Squadriglia*, but he had been temporarily attached to 413ª *Squadriglia*. Having claimed five victories in the CR.32 and CR.42, he had scrambled alone from Gondar to intercept six Gladiators of No 1 Sqn SAAF. Omiccioli was killed, but not before he downed the Gladiator of Lt Smith. Brother of Walter, the top-scoring ace of 54° *Stormo*, Omiccioli received the *Medaglia d'Oro al valor militare*. D'Addetta was killed over Gura in a one-sided battle with Blenheims and their escorting fighters.

The lack of serviceable CR.42s in East Africa by February 1941 meant that the *Regia Aeronautica* could only send up single fighters to oppose

Like CR.42 'ace of aces' Mario Visintini, fellow 412ª *Squadriglia* ace Maresciallo Aroldo Soffritti hailed from 4° *Stormo*. Credited with eight victories, five probables and eleven aircraft destroyed on the ground between 2 February and 4 April 1941, Soffritti's combat career ended when the Italian stronghold of Dessie, in Abyssinia, fell to South African troops on 26 April 1941 (*via Giorgio Apostolo*)

Capitano Guglielmo Chiarini of 366ª *Squadriglia*, 151° *Gruppo* was a permanent air force officer. A bomber pilot in the Spanish Civil War, he had switched to fighters upon his return to Italy. In early June 1940 Chiarini was transferred to Libya, where he joined 82ª *Squadriglia*, 13° *Gruppo*. Over the next few months he proved his worth as a skilled and competent fighter pilot, claiming five individual victories (or possibly four individual and one shared) before the end of 1940, when he was transferred to 151° *Gruppo*. Chiarini was shot down and killed by No 73 Sqn Hurricanes on 4 February 1941. He was later awarded a posthumous *Medaglia d'oro al valor militare* (*Stato Maggiore Aeronautica*)

bombing raids during this period. Indeed, according to the Italian Viceroy there were only 15 airworthy *Falcos* in-theatre at the time.

More CR.42 losses were incurred in North Africa on 4 Feburary when a formation from 151° *Gruppo*, having shot down a Blenheim I of No 45 Sqn, lost the aircraft of Sergente Ezio Masenti – he had been forced to land at Barce airfield with oil starvation. British troops were approaching the area, so as soon as returning pilots reported Masenti's plight, a high-winged Ca.133 took off from Agedabia to look for him. Used as a 'hack' by 151° *Gruppo*, this aircraft was piloted by Maresciallo Giovanni Accorsi of 366ª *Squadriglia*, who was accompanied by engineer 1°Av Mot Callerani. Three CR.42s of 366ª *Squadriglia*, led by ace Tenente Guglielmo Chiarini and including Sergente Antonio Camerini, volunteered to provide an escort for the vulnerable transport.

The Ca.133 was intercepted at low-level by a section of three No 73 Sqn Hurricanes over Barce, Plt Off 'Chips' McColl making short work of the Caproni. Both Accorsi and Callerani were killed. As the CR.42s dived down to assist the doomed transport, the Hurricanes turned to engage them. In the ensuing combat, Chiarini was shot down in flames by ace Plt Off George Goodman, who had targeted a CR.42 that was attacking McColl. Meanwhile, Sergente Antonio Camerini succeeded in damaging a Hurricane that he last saw flying off trailing black smoke. The RAF fighters disappeared after the short combat, leaving the Italians to mourn the loss of two of their most valued pilots. Unbeknown to them, the aircraft flown by Plt Off 'Tiny' Millist, had been shot down in a head-on attack. With his aircraft hit in the engine, Millist had made a forced landing ten miles northeast of Benina. Of Millist's plight, his colleague Plt Off Eiby recalled;

'"Tiny" Millist was a short-service Australian pilot, and when he was shot down by a vintage biplane everyone laughed their bloody heads off. He went in head-on. We were told not to tackle them head-on, but "Tiny" did and got hit in the radiator for his pains.'

Camerini, who had probably shot Millist down, initially claimed the Hurricane as a probable. Both Accorsi and Chiarini were posthumously awarded the *medaglia d'Oro al valor militare*. The unlucky Sergente Maggiore Masenti had to set fire to his fighter and flee Barce with armoured forces, only to be captured during the ensuing Italian retreat.

This last combat, and the death of one of the most popular pilots of the campaign, put a temporary end to Italian fighter operations in North Africa. Three days later at Beda Fomm, the rest of the Italian Army was to be destroyed by the Western Desert Force. The CR.42's time as the *Regia Aeronautica's* main fighter in this theatre had definitely passed.

5 February saw 412ª *Squadriglia* lose two more fighters to No 1 Sqn SAAF, resulting in Sottotenente Giovanni Consoli being killed. Despite these casualties, the unit remained a force to be reckoned with when intercepting Commonwealth reconnaissance and bomber aircraft. This was proven two days later when a Hardy of No 237 Sqn was shot down over the Keren area and two Wellesleys of No 47 Sqn destroyed near Adi Ugri. One of these aircraft may have been claimed by Maresciallo Soffritti, who mistook his opponent for a Blenheim, and the others by Visintini. The top-scoring ace had been promoted to *capitano* on 16 January and received the extremely rare accolade of being mentioned in

CR.42s of 375ª *Squadriglia*, 160° *Gruppo Autonomo* sit lined up at Tirana airfield, in Albania, in May 1941. This well-travelled *gruppo* saw action with its CR.42s in Greece, North Africa and on Sardinia (*Giorgio Apostolo*)

Sottotenente Ugo Drago of 363ª *Squadriglia* smiles for the camera from the cockpit of his CR.42 in early 1940. Drago became a fighter pilot in 1939, and he claimed four victories while flying the CR.42 over the Greek-Albanian front in 1940-41 – he shot down three P.24s and a Battle. Drago went on to claim two more victories flying with the *Regia Aeronautica*, and after the Italian surrender in September 1943, he served with the *ANR*, claiming a further 11 kills. Post-war, he emigrated to Argentina and found employment as a flying instructor. In 1953 he returned home to join the Italian airline *Alitalia*, and was a Boeing 747 captain prior to his retirement (*Archive D'Amico-Valentini*)

War Bulletin 247 of 9 February, which stated 'Capitano Mario Visentini shot down two aircraft on 7 February, gaining his 16th aerial victory'.

The same day that his exploits were being chronicled in print, Visintini led a strafing attack on Agordat airfield, destroying two Wellesleys, two Lysanders and two Hardys. On the 10th, high-scoring ace Capt Ken Driver of No 1 Sqn SAAF was nearly shot down by a CR.42. The Italian fighter doggedly followed him, inflicting damage to his Hurricane's tailplane, elevator, port gun bay, starboard fuel tank and the fairing behind the cockpit. Driver was still able to limp back to Agordat, however. It is possible that Visintini was the pilot who pursued Driver, for his squadronmates credited him with 17 kills.

On 9 February CR.42s of 150° *Gruppo* engaged RAF Gladiators in Greece for the first time in several weeks. Five fighters from No 80 Sqn were intercepted by 16 *Falcos* over Tepelene, and a series of dogfights ensued. Most of the Gladiators were flown by aces, resulting in four CR.42s being lost – Sergenti Maionica and Barolo were killed and Tenente Rovetta and Capitano Travaglini wounded in crash-landings. In return No 80 Sqn had a fighter destroyed, and a second one force-landed.

Later that same day 12 CR.42s from 160° *Gruppo* escorted 18 SM.79s sent to bomb targets near Tepelene. The *Falcos*, led by Tenente Edoardo Crainz, were intercepted by Greek Gladiators and P.24s, and the Italian pilots claimed five victories (one being credited to Crainz) – a Gladiator and a P.24 were downed in actuality. The Greeks made six victory claims, but not a single CR.42 was lost. On the 11th another Greek Gladiator was downed during a strafing attack by 150° *Gruppo* on Yanina airfield.

That same day in East Africa, Mario Visintini led fellow ace Sergente Maggiore Baron and another pilot in a strafing attack on British troops near the Keren mountains. They were intercepted by two Hurricanes, who chased the fighters into thick cloud. Having lost their pursuers, two of the *Falco* pilots landed at a forward strip during the return leg of their flight. Visintini, meanwhile, had made it back to Asmara airfield, where he was told about his wingmen. Immediately taking off again to guide them home through the clouds, he was possibly blown off course by strong winds and crashed into the side of Mount Nefasit. Visintini was killed instantly. He had claimed as many as 17 of the 50+ victories credited to his unit since the start of hostilities in East Africa.

The demolition of 412ª *Squadriglia* continued on the 13th when Capitano Ubaldo Buzzi (possibly flying a CR.32 – the last airworthy example in Eritrea) and Tenente Luigi De Pol were killed in combat with Hurricanes of No 1 Sqn SAAF over Asmara. A third pilot had to make a forced landing. The Italian troops defending the Keren region had, in the meantime, repulsed the initial attack by the 4th Indian Division, bringing almost a month of operations to a halt.

Over Greece, the RAF expeditionary force had been reinforced by the arrival of No 33 Sqn's Hurricanes and No 112 Sqn's Gladiators, while Hurricanes had also started to replace the Gladiators of No 80 Sqn. The CR.42 units now had their work cut out for them, and pilots were wary about going up against the battle-hardened RAF pilots in their Hawker fighters. A far more presentable foe was intercepted by future 363ª *Squadriglia* ace Sottotenente Ugo Drago on 13 February when he downed a lone Greek Battle on a meteorological reconnaissance flight.

Capt Ken Driver claimed his fourth CR.42 destroyed in 11 days over Asmara airfield on 15 February when three No 1 Sqn SAAF Hurricanes saw six *Falcos* over the base. His unnamed victim crashed at high speed.

On 27 February CR.42s of 150° *Gruppo* were in action over Greece once again when 13 fighters intercepted nine Blenheims from Nos 11 and 211 Sqn, escorted by nine Hurricanes from Nos 33 and 80 Sqns. Attacking the aircraft near Valona, the *Falco* pilots badly damaged five bombers (two crash-landed) before the Hurricanes took their toll. Sottotenente Egidio Faltoni and Sergente Osvaldo Bartolaccini were both killed – the RAF pilots claimed seven victories. Considering that no Italian claims were made following this action, it is highly likely that the dead pilots accounted for the downed bombers. If this was indeed the case, then Bartolaccini, who had already claimed three victories over Blenheims, may have become an ace on the day of his death.

The last day of February saw *Falco* pilots embroiled in a sprawling dogfight over Albania that resulted in the RAF claiming its highest single-day kill tally of the Greek campaign. Eight Hurricanes and Gladiators from Nos 33, 80 and 112 Sqns fought 12 G.50s of 24° *Gruppo* and 15 CR.42s of 160° *Gruppo* that were attempting to defend SM.79s and BR.20Ms from attack. The RAF pilots claimed 27 victories, of which 13 were CR.42s – eight Italian aircraft had actually been downed, two of them *Falcos*. In return, the CR.42 pilots claimed two Gladiators and a 'Spitfire' destroyed, but no British fighters had fallen to 160° *Gruppo*.

By early March 1941, only three frontline *gruppi* were still equipped with *Falcos* as their primary fighter – 18° *Gruppo* in North Africa (151° *Gruppo* was recovering and 23° had been rested and was ready to return to Sardinia), 160° in Greece (150° was converting to the C.200) and 156° *Gruppo* in Sicily, which had formed with a number of 23° *Gruppo* pilots that had not gone to Libya. This unit disbanded upon the return of 23° *Gruppo*. Additionally, 3° *Gruppo* was still defending Sardinia, while the autonomous *squadriglie* were fighting on in East Africa.

The decreasing number of CR.42s in the frontline also meant that the opportunities for fighter-vs-fighter action reduced. Nevertheless, units in the Balkans continued to clash with the RAF, and two *Falcos* were lost to Hurricanes on 4 March. Two more from 160° *Gruppo* went down nine days later whilst defending SM.79s, although on this occasion four Gladiators and a Hurricane were claimed destroyed – none were lost.

On 14 March two 160° *Gruppo* machines collided in mid-air whilst trying to down an 815 NAS Swordfish over Corfu, one pilot perishing and the second taking to his parachute.

Second-ranking CR.42 ace Sergente Maggiore Luigi Baron was seriously wounded in combat with Hurricanes from No 1 Sqn SAAF on 25 March 1941. He spent more than two years in hospital before being repatriated to Italy (*Nicola Malizia*)

Tenente Franco Bordoni-Bisleri of 95ª *Squadriglia*, 18° *Gruppo* inspects a bullet-hole in the windscreen of his CR.42 that had been caused by return fire from a Blenheim. Bordoni-Bisleri, who joined the *Regia Aeronautica* in 1937, fought over France and Britain in the CR.42, before finally gaining his first victory (a Blenheim that was possibly shared) on 10 March 1941 in North Africa. He went on to claim a No 73 Sqn Hurricane and three more Blenheims (one of them possibly a No 55 Sqn aircraft) prior to returning to Italy with 95ª *Squadriglia* in August 1941. Bordoni-Bisleri was to claim a further seven victories during the Battle of El Alamein, and then a final kill in the defence of central Italy in 1943. He ended the war as the *Regia Aeronautica's* highest-scoring surviving ace (*Enrico Leproni*)

Bearing a rank pennant, this CR.42 was assigned to Capitano Virginio Teucci of 375ª *Squadriglia*, 160° *Gruppo* (*Enrico Leproni*)

Sergente Maggiore Luigi Gorrini of 85ª *Squadriglia*, 18° *Gruppo* completed two uneventful tours over France and England prior to claiming a Beaufighter shot down in April and a Blenheim in May. His unit then converted to the C.200. Gorrini would claim a total of 15 victories with the *Regia Aeronautica* and four more with the *ANR*. In 1958 he received a *Medaglia d'oro al valor militare* in recognition of his outstanding combat career. Gorrini was the only *ANR* pilot to have been awarded the highest Italian military award after the war for his accomplishments before the Armistice of 8 September 1943 (*Archive D'Amico-Valentini*)

160° *Gruppo* finally enjoyed some success on the night of 15/16 March when a Wellington from No 37 Sqn was downed whilst attempting to bomb Tirana airfield. It was credited to Sergente Maggiore Francesco Penna. The CR.42 subsequently saw little further action in the Balkans following the arrival of the Luftwaffe in late March.

For the *Falco* pilots in East Africa, March really did signal the end of their war. The final attack on the Keren stronghold in the north started on the 15th, by which time the South African Army had reached the centre of Ethiopia. Two days earlier on this southern front, Capitano Romano Palmera and Sergente Eugenio Toninello had been lost to the Hurricanes of No 3 Sqn SAAF shortly after downing the fighter flown by Lt L R Dudley. Toninello was killed and Palmera (a recently-transferred reconnaissance pilot who had shot down a Battle of No 11 Sqn SAAF the previous month) became a PoW.

On the second day of the offensive, Maresciallo Soffritti, in one of the 12 remaining CR.42s on the northern front, was able to down a Wellesley of No 47 Sqn. However, Sottotenente Eugenio Rella was killed by Plt Off P H S Simmonds in a Gladiator from No 237 Sqn that same day. On 18 March 412ª *Squadriglia* attacked Agordat at dawn, destroying a Wellesley and a Hurricane. Later that same day a Hardy of No 237 Sqn was downed by the unit, and on the 19th Maresciallo Soffritti damaged the Hurricane of ace Capt Boyle over the Keren area.

On the 21st, three CR.42s were lost to Hurricanes of No 1 Sqn SAAF over Keren, aces Capt Ken Driver and Lt Robin Pare claiming two of them. Four days later, a Wellesley of No 47 Sqn was shot down, but two more CR.42s were lost to Hurricanes. Sergente Pietro Morlotti lost his life and Sergente Maggiore Luigi Baron was wounded in the left calf. Keren finally fell on the 27th, resulting in 40,000 Italian troops and 300 guns being captured. In the air the surviving CR.42s downed a Vincent.

On the southern front, the remaining fighters of 413ª *Squadriglia* attacked Jijiga airfield at dawn on the 29th, setting three aircraft on fire and damaging three more. A Hurricane was shot down while taking off, but two Italian fighters were lost with their pilots, Sottotenente Francesco Silvano and Sergente Giuseppe Danesin. After downing Blenheim L8433 on 30 March, 412ª *Squadriglia* fought its last battle on 6 April when Tenente Bruno Caldonazzi was killed and Maresciallo Soffritti had to make a force-landing after running out of fuel while chasing a Hurricane.

Only a handful of aircraft remained in East Africa, and by the end of April the last CR.42s had retreated to Gondar, where they resisted until October. Here, they were flown by pilots of 413ª *Squadriglia*, who showed that they were still capable of putting up a fight by downing a Hurricane of No 3 Sqn SAAF in May and a Wellesley of No 47 Sqn in July. The Hurricane was credited to former 410ª *Squadraglia* pilot Sergente Maggiore Antonio Giardinà, who 'made ace' with this success.

Perched on the fuselage of his CR.42 MM5688 '95-9', Sottotenente Franco Bordoni Bisleri flew this aircraft from Mirafiori in the weeks immediately after the Italian declaration of war. His nickname *ROBUR* had been painted on the fighter's headrest – he applied this to all of his fighters (*via Giorgio Apostolo*)

In North Africa, February marked the arrival of the Luftwaffe, and with most RAF units now in Greece, this front remained quiet. The sole CR.42 *gruppi* (151° and 18°) in Libya used this period to equip their fighters with sand filters and bomb racks. By the time the aircraft had been modified, the *Afrika Korps*, together with reinforcements from Italy, was already striking back towards Benghazi. The *Falco* pilots did not participate in this operation, however, being tasked instead with flying second-line point defence missions over harbours and Axis convoys. They were now rarely employed as bomber escorts, this role having been handed over to the more modern G.50s of 2° and 155° *Gruppi*.

This situation persisted until mid-summer, when both *gruppi* were recalled to Italy. They were replaced by two more CR.42 units in the form of 160° and 3° *Gruppi*, whose place on Sardinia had been filled by 23° *Gruppo* in early April. The latter unit, just back from Libya, was re-equipped with CR.42s because of a lack of surplus G.50s.

Despite the relative lack of action in 1941, two outstanding *Falco* pilots emerged from within the ranks of 18° *Gruppo* in North Africa. The first was Sottotenente Franco Bordoni Bisleri of 95ª *Squadriglia*, who had been a talented racing driver pre-war. A participant in the Channel front fiasco, he enjoyed far better fortune in North Africa, where he downed a Blenheim on 10 March with fellow ace Maresciallo Felice Longhi. Bordoni Bisleri claimed a Hurricane on 14 April, followed by another Blenheim three days later. He 'made ace' in June when he was credited with two more Blenheims destroyed. Later flying the C.200 and C.205V in combat, he survived the war with 19 kills to his name.

Also a veteran of the Channel front, fellow 19-victory ace Sergente Maggiore Luigi Gorrini of 85ª *Squadriglia* claimed his first two kills in a CR.42 when he downed a Beaufighter on 16 April and a Blenheim on 29 May.

CR.42s of 394ª *Squadriglia*, 160° *Gruppo Autonomo* taxi out at Devoli, in Albania, in the early spring of 1941. The unit's 'Mussolini's head' badge can be seen just below the cockpit of the aircraft nearest to the camera (*Giorgio Apostolo*)

Giuseppe Mottet was another Spanish Civil War veteran, having claimed four victories during that conflict. In 1939 he transferred to 411ª *Squadriglia, AOI*, with whom he claimed a fifth victory while flying a CR.32. Mottet got his sixth, and last, kill in a CR.42 on 9 July 1941 when he reported downing a Wellesley over Gondar, although this aircraft was in fact only slightly damaged. From 31 October, after the death of his CO Tenente Malavolta, Mottet was the only Italian fighter pilot left in the *AOI*. On 22 November he flew its last CR.42 (MM4033) in an attack on British artillery at Kulkaber, killing Lt Col Ormsby with the only burst fired. This was the *Regia Aeronautica's* last sortie in East Africa. On landing, Mottet destroyed the CR.42 and joined Italian troops, fighting until the surrender five days later (*Roger Juglair*)

Having settled in back on Sardinia, 23° *Gruppo* returned to operations over Malta in early April, but after losing Sergente Giuseppe Sanguettoli to the island's Hurricanes on the 9th, the unit reverted to convoy escort and local defence. Fighter operations over the British fortress were now left in the main to C.200 units. In their new role, the *gruppo's* veterans, still led by Maggiore Falconi, were able to achieve fairly substantial results, downing at least eight Blenheims. Some of these bombers were shared with the C.200s, which were reaching the unit in small numbers. In addition, 23° *Gruppo* pilots accounted for four Wellingtons of the Overseas Air Delivery Unit en route to either Malta or North Africa, as well as a Beaufighter and a Hurricane of No 46 Sqn before year-end.

Prior to its move to North Africa, 3° *Gruppo* had continued its operations from Sardinia, shooting down the Fulmar of 808 NAS ace Lt Cdr Rupert Tillard during attacks on the *Tiger* convoy on 8 May. One of its *squadriglie* (155ª) was chosen to support the Iraqi rebellion in May, and eight fighters flew to Mosul and Kirkuk under the command of Capitano Francesco Sforza. There, on the 29th, they participated in their only combat, losing a *Falco* (whose pilot was captured) to a Gladiator. The flight did, however, shoot down an Audax.

By the summer of 1941 it was clear that the CR.42 was no longer a useful fighter, yet Fiat continued to turn out around 20 examples per month. In the absence of more modern machines, some units like the elite 151° and 160° *Gruppi*, just back in Italy from, respectively, Libya and Albania, were again equipped with the type.

On 27 September, during action over the *Halberd* convoy, eight CR.42s of 24° *Gruppo*, led by Capitano Corrado Santoro (recently returned from East Africa), bounced the Fulmars of 808 NAS. The Italian pilots claimed three destroyed, but only one was actually lost.

Over East Africa on 24 October, one of two airworthy CR.42s in Gondar was sent on a reconnaissance mission. Sottotenente Ildebrando Malavolta was soon intercepted by a SAAF Gladiator flown by Lt L C H Hope, who shot him down. He was the last aviator to fall in combat on that front. The next day Hope dropped a message on Italian positions which read 'a tribute to the pilot of the Fiat – he was a brave man. South African Air Force'. Malavolta received a posthumous *Medaglia d'oro al valor militare*. Having used all of its ammunition in one last strafing attack on 22 November, the final CR.42 was burned to avoid it falling into enemy hands. Gondar fell six days later.

In North Africa, the *Falcos* of 151° *Gruppo* would see action for the last time opposing Operation *Crusader* in November 1941. Hastily redeployed to Libya in response to this Commonwealth offensive, they were chiefly used as fighter-bombers. Nevertheless, the *Falco* pilots proved that they were still more than capable of shooting down Hurricanes when, on the 26th, Capitano Serafini and Sergente Maggiore Camerini claimed the No 33 Sqn machine of Flg Off Bill Winsland over Gialo.

CR.42 '155-14' of 155ª *Squadriglia*, 3° *Gruppo* is seen here bombed up in North Africa in December 1941 (*Archive D'Amico-Valentini*)

Three CR.42AS of 20° *Squadriglia*, 46° *Gruppo* prepare to take off from an airfield in Cyrenaica on a ground attack mission during the autumn of 1942 (*Giorgio Apostolo*)

Two CR.42s from 15° *Stormo* patrol off the Libyan coast. The fighter nearest the camera was assigned to *Stormo* CO, Colonello Raffraele Colacicchi, while the one behind it is from 53ª *Squadriglia*, 46° *Gruppo*. 15° *Stormo* was also employed in the ground attack role in North Africa from September 1942 to February 1943 (*Nicola Malizia*)

The aircraft of 160° *Gruppo* were also still accounting for the odd Blenheim and Beaufighter. An example of the latter from No 272 Sqn fell on 26 November to Sottotenente Giuseppe Cantù of 375ª *Squadriglia*. Although the unit's task was mainly to protect the base at Agedabia, as well as Benghazi harbour, it still suffered losses when encountering Hurricanes, as on 18 November over Gialo when future high-scoring American ace Plt Off Lance Wade of No 33 Sqn claimed his first victories when he shot down the CR.42s of Sergente Alberto Gardelli (who was killed) and the battle-seasoned Sergente Maggiore Luciano Tarantini, who had three and one shared victories to his name.

Nocturnal claims were also made in 1941 by 3° *Gruppo*, which downed a Wellington of No 40 Sqn during a raid on Tripoli on the night of 2/3 November. The aircraft was credited to Tenente Egisto Andalò.

The CR.42 continued to operate in the ground attack role in Libya with 3° *Gruppo* in 1942, while 160° *Gruppo* kept up its convoy escort duty. During widespread combats in the first half of the year, 3° *Gruppo* pilots, in conditions of increasing inferiority (that resulted in some heavy losses), were still able to achieve some aerial victories. For example, on 8 January Sergente Adriano Vezzi of 155ª *Squadriglia* claimed the Kittyhawk of Flg Off Baster from No 3 Sqn RAAF and on 28 March Tenente Andalò downed another Wellington, this time from No 148 Sqn. A rather larger target was claimed by biplanes from 153ª *Squadriglia* on the morning of 27 April when, during a convoy escort mission, they sank the 540-ton submarine HMS *Urge* off the Libyan coast.

At the end of May, 3° *Gruppo* was replaced by 50° *Stormo*, led by Tenente Colonello Vosilla. With its 51 aircraft, this unit was employed during the summer in the actions that led to the capture of Tobruk and

Sergente Floriano Gomiero (unit unknown) climbs into his CR.42. To the left of the pilot's parachute can be seen a rear-view mirror affixed to a wing strut. Although not a standard fitting, such mirrors were occasionally seen on CR.42s in the frontline (*Roger Juglair*)

the first battle of El Alamein. It lost 24 aircraft in action during this period and seven more on the ground, with 17 pilots killed or missing and one captured. 50° *Stormo* was rested at the end of July. As these figures reveal, the *Falco* was no match for the improved flak defences or the Kittyhawks and Hurricanes that were now routinely encountered over the frontline. The *stormo* was quickly reassigned to night harassment operations, its *squadriglie* being reinforced in this role by 101° *Gruppo*, which had arrived in North Africa in August, and by 15° *Stormo* from September.

Equipped with searchlights (seen fitted under the fighter's port wing), this CR.42 was assigned to 167° *Gruppo Autonomo's* 300ª *Squadriglia*, which was created in May 1942 to oversee the noturnal defences of both Rome and Naples (*via Giorgio Apostolo*)

Over the Mediterranean, the CR.42s continued to operate as dive-bombers in aerial operations against the vital summer convoys *Harpoon, Vigorous* and *Pedestal*, bound for Malta. Carrier-based Sea Hurricanes and Fulmars defending the British vessel inflicted heavy losses on the Italian fighters, who claimed very few victories in return.

The only role now suitable for the *Falco* was night interception. This branch of the fighter arm had been ignored by the *Regia Aeronautica* pre-war, but the increasing number of night raids by RAF bombers on Italian cities had forced it to seek a stop-gap solution. The CR.42 was the ideal choice, being docile enough to operate without the help of wireless communications and anything other than basic flight instruments.

While frontline units employed standard day fighters in full moonlight conditions, specialised nightfighter units were also formed. They were issued with radio-equipped, all-black CR.42s that had also had their exhaust pipes and guns fitted with flame suppressors. These fighters gained their first victory on 28 October 1941 when an Albacore of 828 NAS fell near Comiso. A month later a Wellington of Malta-based No 104 Sqn was possibly downed by Sottotenenti Parmeggiani and Calafiore of 376ª *Squadriglia* over Naples. Another Wellington of No 40 Sqn was definitely destroyed near Naples by Maresciallo Joseph Vincent Patriarca of 356ª *Squadriglia,* 21° *Gruppo* on the night of 5/6 December.

A well-known ace who claimed a nocturnal *Falco* victory was Tenente Giulio Reiner, who scored a trio of CR.42 kills in North Africa in 1940-41. He downed a Wellington of No 40 Sqn on the night of 25/26 August 1942 over Fuka in a standard CR.42 borrowed from 101° *Gruppo*.

Although the nightfighter units gradually received more modern machines, the CR.42s remained one of the most effective nocturnal hunters in the Italian arsenal. Indeed, they demonstrated this on the night of 21 November 1942 when Capitano Giovanni Scagliarini of 233ª *Squadriglia CN* downed a Halifax of No 76 Sqn over Turin. This proved to be the very last victory scored by an Italian CR.42. The final claim, however, was to be made the following year during the night of 14/15 February, when Tenente Cesare Balli of 41° *Stormo CN* inflicted serious damage on a Lancaster over Milan. The bomber managed to return to base, albeit with one engine knocked out and two crewmen wounded.

Capitano Vittorio Pezzé (left) and Sergente Alberto Bottazzi (right) give instruction to students in front of a CR.42 at the *Scuola Caccia* (fighter school) at Gorizia in 1942. Pezzé was one of Italy's leading aerobatic pilots in the 1930s, and he duly became CO of 73ª *Squadriglia*. He claimed two shared kills in the CR.42 in North Africa prior to being repatriated due to illness in October 1940. Bottazzi claimed a share in a Wellington downed on the night of 22 October while serving with 94ª *Squadriglia*. He also instructed at the *Scuola Caccia* during 1942-43 (*Fulvio Chianese – Associazione Culturale 4° Stormo di Gorizia*)

UNDER OTHER FLAGS

In late September 1939 a Belgian purchasing mission arrived in Turin to negotiate the acquisition of 40 CR.42s to meet the urgent re-equipment needs of its *Aéronautique Militaire's IIème Group de Chasse* (2nd Fighter Group, comprising the *3ème* and *4ème Escadrilles*), which was seeking to replace its ageing Fairey Fireflies. The Italians demanded a high price for the *Falcos*, but negotiations were completed by December. The first CR.42s arrived at the Evere *Établissements Généraux de l'Aéronautique Militaire* for assembly on 6 March 1940, still in Italian camouflage.

Each *Escadrille* was to receive 15 fighters, assigned the serials R.1 to R.30, with the remaining aircraft were intended to serve as attrition replacements. The first unit to convert to the CR.42 was the *3ème Escadrille*, and both had completed their transition by the end of April. *IIème Group de Chasse*, based at Nivelles, south of Brussels, was led by Maj Jacques Lamarche. Its two *escadrilles* used World War 1 ace Willy Coppens' *cocotte* (paper duck) insignia, in red for 3/II and white for 4/II.

Belgian CR.42s became the first examples of the Fiat fighter to fire their guns in anger when they were involved in the brief but vain attempt made by the small *Aéronautique Militaire* to oppose the might of the German *blitzkrieg*, launched on 10 May 1940. By then the Belgians had accepted between 24 and 27 of the 40 CR.42s on order. The *3ème Escadrille* of the *IIème Group de Chasse*, which was commanded by Cne Jean de Callataÿ, had achieved its full 15-aircraft strength just days before Belgium was invaded. However, only nine CR.42s had been taken on charge by the other component unit, the *4ème Escadrille*, which was commanded by Cne Thiery d'Huart.

At 0100 hrs on 10 May, Nivelles airfield was alerted to the possibility of a German attack. *IIème* was to be transferred before dawn to Field No 22 at Brustem, close to the German border. At sunrise most of the operational CR.42s were ready for take-off, and the fighters commenced their departure in groups of three at 0445 hrs. The first to go was R.43 (formerly R.13), flown by Maj Lamarche, who led the first formation. The departure was completed without incident, but as the first fighters were about to land at Brustem at 0505 hrs, enemy aircraft were sighted to the east. Some of the pilots were eager to attack, but they received orders to land. 1Sgt Marcel Michotte (in R.30) of the *4ème Escadrille*

CR.42 R.21 of 4/II/1 *Aé* displays the unit's white *cocotte* (paper duck) insignia. This aircraft was damaged during the German attack on Nivelles on 10 May 1940, when Ju 87Bs from I./St.G.2 attacked the airfield. R.21 was duly moved into a hangar and destroyed at the end of May (*Peter Taghon*)

During the evacuation of Nivelles at dawn on 10 May 1940, 1Sgt Marcel Michotte of 4/II/1 *Aé* nosed over in R.30 while landing at Brustem. The aircraft was not badly damaged, but it fell victim to the lightning advance of German troops across Belgium and was never repaired. Michotte escaped unhurt, and claimed to have damaged a Bf 109E four days later when five Belgian CR.42s clashed with 8./JG 3 near Fleurus (*Marco Gargari*)

ground-looped and his aircraft ended up on its nose with a bent propeller. It could not be repaired at Brustem and was written off.

As the last aircraft were preparing to land, the flight led by Cne de Callataÿ spotted Ju 52/3ms over Tongres. The transports were from 17./KGzbV.5, and they had been tasked with dropping dummy parachutists in the area as a diversion for the main assault. De Callataÿ and his two wingmen, Sgt Joseph Van Molkot and Cpl Marcel Hansel, went after the tri-motored transports, and Callataÿ scored hits on one near Alken at 0530 hrs. This aircraft crash-landed at Maastricht.

The Belgian pilots were immediately set upon by the escorting Bf 109Es from I./JG 1 and they became separated. Van Molkot landed at Brustem, while de Callataÿ and Hansel returned to Nivelles, as they believed Brustem had been bombed. De Callataÿ's claim for a Ju52/3m was not officially confirmed.

Meanwhile, the mechanics at Nivelles had been trying to get the three remaining CR.42s at the airfield ready for action – 1Sgt Marcel Sans finally took off in one of the fighters at 0515 hrs. Sous-Lt Yves Duomonceau was preparing to following him a few minutes later when the airfield was attacked by Ju 87Bs from 4./StG 2. Despite this, he managed to get airborne in R.4, but could not attack the Stukas because of malfunctioning machine guns. The attack caused considerable damage to the base, although it did not prevent Cne de Callataÿ and Cpl Hansel from landing there once the Ju 87s had departed. Minutes after taxiing in, de Callataÿ's aircraft (R.2) and two other CR.42s (R.21 and R.27) were damaged when a time-delayed bomb exploded nearby. Callataÿ immediately jumped into another CR.42 and returned to Brustem.

Constant fighter cover was ordered from 0555 hrs in an atempt to prevent the airfield from being attacked by Bf 109Es and Bf 110C/Ds. Two patrols of three CR.42s were duly deployed. When the first patrol readied itself for take-off, 1Sgt Sans' CR.42 refused to start, so Lt Charles Goffin and 1Sgt Roger Delannay took off without him. At 0625 hrs, over Brustem, the fighters encountered 10-15 Bf 109Es from I./JG 1 and Delannay's aircraft was downed. The pilot bailed out unscathed, but as he descended he was mortally wounded by groundfire. Rushed to Sint-Trudostraat hospital in St Trond, Delannay succumbed to his wounds.

Goffin had better luck, damaging a Bf 109E that left the fray trailing a plume of smoke at 0630 hrs. This aircraft was flown by Leutnant E Dutel of 2./JG 1, who was forced to bail out over Aix-la-Chapelle (Aachen). Dutel had been flying with a group of 19 Bf 109Es escorting 40 Ju 52/3ms in the St Trond/Tongres area. The German fighter pilots reported encountering five 'Gladiators', one of which was shot down.

The second patrol, consisting of future ace Sous-Lt Jean Offenberg and 1Sgts Jean Maes and Alexis Jottard, attacked a Do 17Z escorted by Bf 109Es from I./JG 1 at 0630 hrs. Even before Offenberg had given the attack signal, 1Sgt Maes had placed his aircraft behind the Dornier and opened fire. He watched it losing altitude, and when he followed it he dived too steeply and suffered a blackout. Having lost sight of the German bombers, Maes returned to base and claimed a Do 17Z damaged. While the latter was attacking the bomber, Offenberg and Jottard were doing their best to keep the escorting Bf 109Es at bay.

On his way back to Brustem, Offenberg twice met lone Do 17Zs. On the first occasion he reported damaging the bomber, but on the second encounter he was more successful. Offenberg lost sight of his target after setting its left engine on fire with two well-aimed bursts. Neither Offenberg's nor Maes' claims were officially confirmed, however. It is likely that they had encountered Do 17Zs from II./KG 77, as the unit lost a Dornier from 5. *Staffel*, which crashed near Vroenhoven. This aircraft was listed in German records as having been downed by flak, but it is possible that it was attacked by Offenberg and/or Maes.

Shortly after 0900 hrs, three CR.42s from 3/II/2 *Aé*, flown by Sous-Lt Marcel Siraut and 1Sgts Marcel Sans and Emile de Moerlose, departed Brustem on an escort mission for a Renard R.31 from *Escadrille* 9/V/1 that had been tasked with reconnoitring Zuid-Willemsvaart. The fighters met the Renard over Brustem at 0950 hrs, and in spite of a flak barrage, they proceeded to fly over Hasselt towards Maaseik. The mission was completed without incident and the Fiats returned to base at 1025 hrs.

Lt Dumonceau, who had taken off from Nivelles in the midst of the Stuka attack, was reunited with his unit at Brustem at 1120 hrs. Ninety minutes later, *Escadrille* VI/1 called for fighters to escort a reconnaissance flight over the bridges spanning the Albert Canal. At 1330 hrs three CR.42s from 3/II/2 *Aé* duly took off, piloted by Lt Werner de Mérode, Adj Elie Français and Sous-Lt Jean Moreau. Once again, this reconnaissance mission was flown without incident. At 1410 hrs, before de Mérode's patrol had returned, orders arrived at Brustem for yet another escort mission for a Renard from *Escadrille* V/1. This time the fighters would be led by Cne de Callataÿ.

At 1415 hrs, as the pilots were climbing into their cockpits, a German reconnaissance aircraft flew directly over Brustem. Immediately, Maj Lamarche ordered the aircraft to be dispersed in the undergrowth. There was not enough time to hide them all, however, with only the CR.42s from 4/II/2 *Aé* being covered. At 1440 hrs, two hedge-hopping Bf 109Es strafed the field and scored strikes on two *Falcos*.

At around the same time Lt de Mérode, returning from his escort mission, spotted a Do 17 (probably the one that had flown over the field) and he claimed to have shot it down in flames near Waremme at 1440 hrs. This was a Do 17P from 2(F)./123, and it belly-landed at Mönchengladbach. This claim was not officially credited to de Mérode until 1947. Mérode's patrol landed at 1515 hrs.

Ten minutes later the sky over Brustem was filled with Ju 87Bs from I./StG 2, which proceeded to wreak havoc. Fourteen CR.42s out of a total of 22 were put out of action, with the only survivors being the eight aircraft of 4/II/2 *Aé* that had been hastily hidden. Cne d'Huart transferred some of his *Falcos* to *Cne* de Callataÿ, who had lost all of his.

The following day the surviving CR.42s were transferred to Grimberg, north of Brussels, as German reconnaissance aircraft were now constantly

Sous-Lt Jean Offenberg of 4/II/2 *Aé* poses in front of one of the unit's CR.42s. Offenberg claimed one victory with the *Falco* when he reported shooting down a Do 17 near Tongeren on 10 May 1940. After the Belgian surrender, he and 1Sgt Alexis Jottard flew two Caudron Simouns to Montpelier on 19 June, and then onto Algeria the next day, where they joined the Belgian flying school that had been set up at Oujda. Finding morale low here, they attempted, unsuccessfully, to obtain an aircraft to fly to Gibraltar. Instead, they took a train to Casablanca and sailed on the cargo ship *Djebel Druse* to Gibraltar. The pilots eventually made it to England on the *Har Sion* in July, reaching Liverpool on the 16th. Offenberg took part in the latter stages of the Battle of Britain, flying Hurricanes with No 145 Sqn. During his time with this unit he claimed three victories, before being transferred to Spitfire-equipped No 609 Sqn. Offenberg claimed one additional kill with this unit on 7 July 1941 to take his total to five. While on a training flight with a new pilot on 22 January 1942, he was subjected to a mock attack by a No 92 Sqn Spifire, but the aircraft collided and the tail of Offenberg's machine was sliced off. It dived vertically into the ground and Offenberg was killed (*Peter Taghon*)

Burned-out Belgian CR.42s litter the landing ground at Brustem. The aircraft nearest the camera displays the construction number N.230 on its rear fuselage, while the one in the background is R.4 of 3/II/1 *Aé*. During the afternoon of 10 May 1940, the *IIème Group de Chasse* lost 14 out of a total of 22 CR.42s when they were surprised by Stukas. The 3/II/2 *Aé* was practically wiped out, and only eight CR.42s from 4/II/2 *Aé*, which had been hidden in the adjacent undergrowth, survived (*Marco Gargari*)

overflying Brustem. The move commenced at 1000 hrs when Lamarche ordered two Fiats up to provide cover. Three more fighters (piloted by Offenberg, Jottard and Maes) were being prepared for take-off when a formation of six Do 17Zs from KG 77 was sighted over the airfield. They were immediately attacked by the CR.42s that were already airborne, while the remaining fighters took off. The Dorniers bombed the airfield, and also St-Trond, before disappearing into the clouds. According to Lamarche, the patrol claimed one Do 17, but this has never been officially confirmed, and is not verified by German records either.

All eight remaining CR.42s reached Grimberg at 1100 hrs. A little over four hours later they received new orders to move to airfield No 31 (Nieuwkerken-Waas) in northern Belgium. During the unit's short stay at Grimberg, a pilot from the *Etablissements Aé* landed with a repaired CR.42. Eight fighters flew to Nieuwkerken-Waas, while the ninth, flown by Sgt Richard, was slightly damaged during take-off and it remained at the base until the following day. The *Falcos* landed at Nieuwkerken-Waas at 1820 hrs, where they joined the French reconnaissance and army observation unit GAO 502, equipped with Potez 63.11s.

The CR.42 pilots flew just two sorties on 13 May as the unit attempted to bed in at its new base. The following day the *IIème Group* sent its serviceable aircraft into action to cover the retreat of the French 7th *Armée* from Fleurus. At 1130 hrs six CR.42s (flown by Cne de Callataÿ, Sous-Lts Albert Oger and André Papeians de Morchoven, Adj Elie Français and 1Sgts Marcel Michotte and Willy de Moerloose) took off. Moerlose left the flight during the patrol to chase a Do 17, which he claimed to have damaged. Over Fleurus at 1300 hrs, the remaining CR.42s were intercepted by Bf 109Es from 8./JG 3. During the ensuing combat one 'Emil' was claimed as destroyed by Callataÿ and Michotte damaged another. Conversely, 8./JG 3 claimed five of the Fiats downed following this combat. In reality, Français' fighter had been damaged, and he made a forced landing at Nivelles. A second CR.42 was also shot up, but it was able to return to base. The fighter was not repaired, however. For its part, 8./JG 3 sustained no losses in this combat.

At 1242 hrs on 15 May four CR.42s took off to escort Fox O.38 on a reconnaissance mission over Lierre-Onze, Liewve and Vrouw-Wavre. They met their charge over Grimberg, but one of the Fiats (flown by Cne Jo Devroy) was forced to return to base with engine trouble. The three remaining CR.42s (Lt Goffin, Sous-Lt Moreau and 1Sgt De Valck) remained to provide the escort. Southeast of Malines, the formation was attacked by nine Bf 109Es from 8./JG 3. Goffin claimed to have shot one of them down over Mechelen at 1320 hrs, and although this claim is indeed officially credited to him, it is not verified by German records.

That the evening the decision was taken to evacuate the unit to France. At 0350 hrs on 16 May the six remaining CR.42s, accompanied by some

Fairey Fireflies, took off for Aeltre. Two non-operational *Falcos* were flown to Zwevezele to receive new propeller blades later that same day.

II/2 Aé's stay at Aeltre was brief, for at 1430 hrs on the 16th it received orders to move to Norrent-Fontes. Four hours later, the CR.42s took off in two groups of three to protect the slower Fireflies. The six fighters were flown by Cne Devroy, Sous-Lts Offenberg and Moureau, 1Sgts Jottard and Maes and Cpl Hansel. They crossed the French border at Houplines and all landed safely at Norrent-Fontes at 1930 hrs. The pilots were rested on 17 May, but in the evening they were informed that the CR.42s were to go to Montpellier while the Fireflies headed for Caen.

At 1030 hrs on the 18th, the six CR.42s took off, led by Callataÿ, and landed at Chartres. The following afternoon 1Sgts Maes and Robert Dizelle flew their first patrol over the surrounding area. Shortly after they landed the airfield was attacked by Do 17Zs, and Maes' R.26 was destroyed. Further patrols were flown over Chartes between 20-26 May. After a day of rest, the pilots received news of the unconditional Belgian surrender on the 28th. Nevertheless, they all decided to continue the fight, and Offenberg, Goffin and Maes flew two patrols during the day.

At 1330 hrs on 3 June, four CR.42s flown by Lt Goffin, Sous-Lt Dumonceau, 1Sgt Jottard and Cpl Hansel were scrambled, together with Chartres' Czech-manned patrol, to intercept enemy bombers. They attacked a dozen Do 17Zs at 14,500-16,000 ft at 1340 hrs. Goffin twice targeted a bomber on the formation's left hand side and returned to claim it as damaged. Jottard fired 700 rounds of ammunition and also claimed to have damaged one of the attackers, which was seen trailing black and white smoke. It is likely that the CR.42s had been in combat with Do 17Zs from KG 76. This unit reported two aircraft lost and five damaged south of Ham during raids on Chartres airfield at 1310 hrs and Claye-Souilly airfield at 1330 hrs. Two CR.42s (R.23 and R.28) were damaged on the ground during the attack.

The following days proved to be remarkably devoid of action, but on 9 June four CR.42s were scrambled twice. By the 11th the German advance was closing in on Chartres, forcing the airfield to be evacuated. The remaining CR.42s were to be flown to Bordeaux-Mérignac after Offenberg, Jottard and Maes had flown a final patrol from Chartres in the morning. That afternoon, the five Belgian fighters departed, flown by Offenberg and Cpls Baldt, Hubert, Delperdange and Geyssens.

Sous-Lt Moureau subsequently damaged an enemy reconnaissance aircraft near Chartres at 1340 hrs on 15 June, but this claim remains unconfirmed. Two days later the five Fiats were ordered to Montpellier. They were flown by 1Sgts De Valck and Maes and Cpls Bladt, Hubert and Geyssens, but bad weather delayed their arrival until the 18th. The Belgian fighters were not used again, and France surrendered on 22 June, the armistice taking effect at 0135 hrs on the 25th.

Between 10 May and 22 June, the CR.42s of the *Aéronautique Militaire* had flown 224 sorties, taken part in 25 dogfights and claimed six victories. The remaining Belgian pilots returned home by lorry and were demobilised at Diest on 20 August. Seven days later, the five remaining CR.42s (R.24, R.29, R.31, R.32 and R.33) were handed over to the Germans. Their ultimate fate remains unknown. Several Belgian *Falco* pilots escaped to the UK and joined the RAF, among them

Charles Goffin poses for the camera while seated in the cockpit of a USAAF Spitfire in 1944. While serving in the 3/II/2 *Aé*, he claimed his only two CR.42 victories, on 10 and 15 May 1940. Both claims are officially confirmed. He intercepted a bomber on 3 June and reportedly damaged it, but this claim is not officially recognised. Goffin escaped from occupied Belgium in January 1941 and made his way to the UK, where he later flew with the 14th Photographic Squadron, 7th Photo Reconnaissance Group, Eighth Air Force, USAAF. Completing his first sortie on 26 March 1944, Goffin was killed on 8 September 1944 while flying Spitfire Mk XI MB952 during a mapping reconnaissance mission. He was undertaking his 33rd sortie with the unit at the time (*Scott Blyth*)

Offenberg (killed in a flying accident on 22 January 1942, having scored five and two shared victories), Jottard (killed in action on 27 October 1940), de Callataÿ, de Mérode, Bladt and Delperdange. Goffin joined the USAAF in 1942, but was killed in action on 8 August 1944.

EASTERN FRONT

Although the Belgian CR.42s were the first of their type to go into action, the Fiat fighter's first foreign customer was Hungary. The *Magyar Királyi Honvéd Légierö* (MKHL – Royal Hungarian Air Arm) had placed an order for 18 aircraft during the summer of 1938, despite being fully aware that the CR.42 was conceptually outdated. The MKHL considered the rapid re-equipment of its fighter component to be of more importance at the time.

The fighters arrived in Hungary between 16 June and 20 November 1939, the 1. *vadász ezred* (1st Fighter Regiment) commencing its conversion from the CR.32 as soon as the first CR.42s were delivered. The 1/3. *Kör ász vadászszázad* (Ace of Hearts Squadron) was the first to receive *Falcos*, and it also suffered the first fatality when szakaszvezetö Béla Simon crashed at Mátyásföld in V.207 on 4 October 1939.

The following month Hungary ordered an additional 50 CR.42s, and they arrived in 1940. The 1. *vadász ezred's* two two-squadron component groups, 1./I *osztály* (fighter group) at Budapest's Mátyásföld airfield (it later moved to Kolozsvár-Szamosfalva, where it was re-designated 2/II. *osztály*) and 1./II *osztály*, also at Mátyásföld, had received their full complement of fighters by the late spring. In 1942 the Hungarians and the Italians exchanged a captured Yugoslavian SM.79 for two more CR.42s, bringing the total number of *Falcos* flown by the MKHL to 70.

When a special Air Force Brigade was formed in the spring of 1941 to accompany the Hungarian Fast Corps that was to participate in the June assault on the Soviet Union (Hungary declared war on the USSR on 27 June), CR.42s formed its principal fighter element.

At 0800 hrs on 27 June, the MKHL launched its first air attack on Soviet targets when a force of 30 bombers, comprising Ju 86K-2s of the 4/3. and 4/4. *bombázószázad* (bomber squadron) and Ca.135bis of the 3/5. *bombázószázad*, attacked targets in Stanislav. They were escorted by nine CR.42s from the 2/3. *'Ricsi' vadászszázad* of 2./II *osztály*, and were

The freshly-arrived, silver-painted V.203 of the 1/3. *'Kör Ász' vadászszázad*, seen here in early autumn 1939. The 1/3. *vadászszázad* was the first Hungarian unit to be equipped with CR.42s *(Csaba Becze Archive)*

led by százados vitéz Aladár Szobránczy. After the bombers had done their work, the fighters strafed targets of opportunity in the area.

V.210 of the 1/3. **'*Kör Ász*' *vadászszázad*, seen here in the winter of 1939-40, displays the early camouflage scheme applied to Hungarian CR.42s. This aircraft was frequently used by *főhadnagy* György Ujszászy, who used it to claim two Soviet 'I-17s' (LaGG-3s or MiG-3s) over Uljanovka on 27 August 1941. Later, he returned to the Eastern Front and scored five more victories while flying the Bf 109F in 1943. Ujszászy's last kills came on 13 April 1944 when he claimed a share in a USAAF B-24, which he credited to his wingman and is thus not included in his overall tally. After the war Ujszászy moved to the USA (*Csaba Becze Archive*)**

It was at this point that örmester Arpád Kertész became lost in dense cloud, and when he finally broke through the overcast he sighted a reconnaissance aircraft. As he approached, its gunner opened fire, enabling Kertész to identify the aeroplane as a Soviet Polikarpov R-5. After a short exchange of fire, the Soviet machine burst into flames. Kertész turned back for his base, flying on instruments, but after a while his fuel ran low and he decided to land. Fortunately for him he found himself among Rumanian troops, although it took him more than a week to rejoin his unit.

During the same mission, the 2/3. *'Ricsi' vadászszázad* had lost CR.42 V.217 when zászlós László Kázár was downed by anti-aircraft fire. He made a forced landing, and after setting fire to his personal mount for two years, he returned to base after 16 days behind enemy lines. Kázár was helped in his escape by local Ukrainian anti-Communist guerrillas.

Despite poor weather conditions over the sub-Carpathian region on 29 June, Hungarian aircraft flew several combat missions. A total of 25 Ju 86K-2 and Ca.135bis bombers, escorted by CR.42s, targeted Striy. This was the last action of a two-day strategic bombing offensive against Soviet rear area targets undertaken in retaliation for the bombing of Kassa. While returning from the mission, CR.42 V.245 of the 2/3. *vadászszázad*, flown by future ace főhadnagy László Pottyondy, force-landed. The fighter overturned and was badly damaged, although the pilot escaped uninjured.

On 8 July the 2/3. *vadászszázad* moved from its advanced base at Bustyaháza, in Hungary, to a captured Soviet airfield five miles from Kolomea. That same day the 2/4. *Nyil vadászszázad* of the 2./II *vadászosztály* suffered the loss of three CR.42s (V.253, V.254 and V.255) in bad weather over the Carpathian Mountains. Section leader hadnagy Pál Irányi hit a tree but survived, and eventually became an ace. Szakaszvezetö Antal Nébli (in V.253) was not so lucky, being killed when he crashed northeast of Dora. The third pilot, szakaszvezetö Endre Bajcsy, bailed out and broke his hip when he landed in rough terrain.

On 10 July the 2/3. *'Ricsi' vadászszázad* moved its nine CR.42s to Yezierzany landing ground. The following day, *'hadnagy Vámos'* section from the 2/3. *'Ricsi' vadászszázad* provided air cover for advancing units of the Hungarian Fast Corps. There were no enemy aircraft in the air, but not wishing to return without firing their guns, the three Fiats attacked and dispersed a retreating Soviet column in the Smotricz area. Almost immediately, five Soviet I-16 *Rata* fighters appeared, and in the ensuing dogfight, the section shot one down and severely damaged another. The remaining three Soviet aircraft were sent fleeing eastwards. Upon returning to base, hadapród örmester Béla Dikó of the 2/3. *vadászszázad*

Two Hungarian CR.42s from the 1/3. *'Kör ász' vadászszázad* soak up the sun on the Eastern Front. 1/3. *vadászszázad* was the *MKHL's* main fighter unit during the initial phase of the attack on the USSR, serving on this front from 13 July to 26 November 1941. It claimed 17 kills and one probable during 114 missions and 447 individual combat sorties, while losing two pilots and two aircraft (*D Bernád collection*)

Főhadnagy Aladár Negró (centre) claimed two Slovakian B.534s destroyed near Szobránc on 24 March 1939 while flying a CR.32. In 1940 Negró changed his surname to Szobránczy in honour of his claim. He served as a százados and commander of the 2/3. *'Ricsi' vadászszázad,* operating CR.42s in the summer and autumn of 1941 on the Eastern Front. On 12 July 1941 he made a single claim in the CR.42 when he reported downing an I-16. He is seen with his men after that combat (*Csaba Becze Archive*)

somersaulted CR.42 V.257 at Stanislav and was injured. He was taken to hospital, while his aircraft required extensive repairs.

On the 12th *alezredes* Béla Orosz, commander of the air contingent attached to the Fast Corps, ordered százados Aladár Szobránczy, commander of the 2/3. *vadászszázad,* to provide escort for two short-range reconnaissance squadrons that were to bomb an enemy transport assembly point west of Zwanczyk. Szobránczy, föhadnagy László Pottyondy, hadnagy Győző Vámos (in CR.42 V.265) and szakaszvezetös Péter Soós and János Balogh took off at 1000 hrs and soon joined the formation of Weiss Manfred WM 21 Sólyom biplanes from the VIIth and Xth *közelfelderítö-század.*

On the way to the target Szobránczy sighted three twin-engined Soviet bombers. As the Fiats dived on them, seven I-16s suddenly appeared and engaged the Hungarian biplanes. Szobránczy targeted a fighter, and soon saw his tracers hitting its cockpit. The machine began to trail thick smoke, and it hit the ground west of Zvanchyk. Pottyondy also attacked an I-16 but, at the same time, he too found himself being tailed by a second *Rata.* When he spotted that Soós had latched onto his victim-to-be, Pottyondy found himself free to concentrate on his attacker.

Managing to get behind the Russian fighter, his bullets tore pieces off its fuselage. The enemy pilot then steadied his aircraft, only to fly into the fire of the oncoming Vámos. The two machines raced towards each other and collided head-on. Pottyondy saw two parachutes floating down before being attacked by another I-16. Again eventually working his way behind his opponent, the Hungarian first hit the tail of his quarry with a burst of fire and then moved forwards to the section of fuselage between the engine and the cockpit. Having been mortally hit, the I-16 spun out of control towards the ground near Dunayevtsy.

Meanwhile, the WM 21s had completed their task and turned for home. Despite being fired upon from the ground, all but one returned. Pottyondy and Balogh, who had also shot down an I-16, were the last to leave the area, yet they were the first back in Kolomea. Soon, Soós arrived and reported that he too had scored a victory. However, Vámos, seen to bail out after the collision, and Szobránczy were still missing.

After shooting down his opponent and watching Vámos' collision, Szobránczy had decided to try to find his downed squadronmate. Circling around the parachute, he noticed that Vámos was hanging motionless. When his body hit the treetops, a Russian patrol appeared at the edge of the wood. Szobránczy halted their advance with a few well-aimed bursts. Looking around, he saw a meadow along the southeast edge of the forest and put his Fiat down. The machine came to a halt after about 250 ft, but its undercarriage sank into the soft ground. A group of horsemen then appeared galloping towards him and Szobránczy drew his pistol. To his great relief it was not needed for they were Hungarian hussars who had watched his landing.

Szobránczy detailed a hussar to guard the aircraft, mounted his horse and began to search for Vámos with the remaining cavalrymen. They soon found his parachute, but it took a further 90 minutes to find the pilot – asleep in an abandoned forester's hut! Vámos explained that he had lost consciousness on bailing out and could not remember pulling the ripcord. He came to when he hit the trees. Fired on near the forest, he went farther into the woods until he saw the hut, where, exhausted, he fell into a deep sleep. In the meantime, a Hungarian armoured unit had reached the scene and towed the *Falco* onto solid ground.

In all, the 2/3. *vadászszázad* claimed five kills during the day without loss to its pilots. According to some sources, the I-16 that collided with Vámos was credited to Pottyondy as an unconfirmed victory, as he had fired at it before the collision. It appears that the unit's opponents had been SB bombers from 132 SBAP and I-16s from 168 IAP. The former reported that at noon six SBs had bombed Axis tanks at Dunayevtsy, and that three others had attacked more tanks at Shatava. The report added;

'Near Shatava, six enemy sesquiplane fighters (probably Hungarian CR.42s) attempted to attack our bombers but were driven away by our fighters, which arrived just in time. During the hurried withdrawal, two enemy aircraft collided and crashed to the ground in flames.'

Returning from the target, the bombers were attacked by six Bf 109s north of Dunayevtsy. The I-16 *zveno* from 168 IAP, tasked with escort duties, barred the way to the bombers and forced them into a dogfight. The combat lasted 15 minutes. Meanwhile, the bombers had completed their mission and left. Three fighters, flown by Kapitan Pilshchikov, Starshiy Leytenant Shurmin and Leytenant Klimenko, failed to return. A parachute was observed, but the pilot's identity was not established.

Next morning, a message arrived from Kapitan Pilshchikov. He informed his headquarters that his *zveno* had clashed with three 'Fiat' aircraft in the Dunayevtsy and Solobkovtsy areas. The 'Fiats' were followed by four others, which also joined the fight. Pilshchikov shot down one of them during the first attack. However, a second came at him in a frontal attack, damaging the engine of his I-16. He had to disengage from combat and, upon reaching friendly territory, he landed near Bar. The fighter was burned out and the pilot rejoined his unit several days later.

Three pilots of 2/3. *'Ricsi' vadászszázad* are seen in front of one of their CR.42s on 12 July 1941. On this day the unit claimed five Soviet I-16s while losing one CR.42. After the combat, *százados* Aladár Szobránczy and *hadnagy* Gyözö Vámos were decorated with the bronze *Signum Laudis*, while *föhadnagy* László Pottyondy received the silver *Signum Laudis*. The 2/3. *vadászszázad* was relieved by the 1/3. *vadászszázad* the next day, the former unit returning to its base at Kolozsvár. Its pilots claimed seven victories during this short period, and they were to be back on the Eastern Front by 1944 (*D Bernád collection*)

Százados László Tomor, CO of the 1/3. *'Kör ász' vadászszázad*, leans on the wingtip of his V.206 at Yezierzany airfield in July 1941. The 1/3. *vadászszázad* arrived at this airfield on 13 July to relieve the 2/3. *'Ricsi' vadászszázad* as the *MKHL's* main fighter unit on the Eastern Front (*Csaba Becze Archive*)

Several hours after being posted missing, Leytenant Klimenko returned to base. He reported that he had fought until his I-16 had run out of fuel. In the end, he had successfully landed 6.25 miles south of Dorozhnya. However, he had to burn his aircraft as the area had already been abandoned by Soviet troops. He also reported that, besides the 'Fiat' shot down by Pilshchikov, he had seen a second one falling in flames. He assumed that it had been brought down by Starshiy Leytenant Shurmin. It is believed that he rammed a CR.42 near Strybiz and was killed in the process. In all, 168 IAP lost six I-16s and four pilots during the day.

A dozen CR.42s of the 1/3. *'Kör ász' vadászszázad*, under the command of százados László Tomor, were redeployed to Kolomea (Kolomiya) and advanced to the landing ground at Yezierzany on 13 July. The 2/3. *'Ricsi' vadászszázad* was relieved at this point and sent back to its base at Kolozsvár. The unit's pilots had claimed seven victories during this short period. Subsequently returning to the Eastern Front in late 1942 equipped with Bf 109F/Gs, the Hungarian fighter pilots further distinguished themselves in combat.

Meanwhile, the CR.42s of the 1/3. *vadászszázad* were accompanying the Air Force Brigade deeper into the Soviet Union, and between 14-19 July they flew several reconnaissance and escort sorties.

On 20 July 12 CR.42s of the 1/3. *vadászszázad* moved 70 miles eastwards to Bar. There, the unit shared the airfield with a German short-range reconnaissance squadron and a Slovakian Avia B.534 fighter unit. Százados László Tomor, CO of the 1/3. *Vadászszázad*, took off from Bar with four other CR.42s on the 22nd to reconnoitre the area between Braclav, Bersady, Tulchyn and Dzhurin. During this mission, they attacked and strafed enemy troop columns and armour. Ground fire was intense and only one Fiat escaped unscathed. Százados Tomor was wounded in five different places, but he still returned to base.

On 22 July 1941 százados László Tomor, CO of the 1/3. *vadászszázad*, strafed enemy troop and armoured columns in company with four other CR.42 pilots. Tomor's V.206 was hit in several places, and it was duly patched up with red stars painted over the grey patches (*G Punka collection*)

On 23 July the CR.42s of the 1/3. *vadászszázad* moved to Sutysk and then on to Annopol five days later, before flying to Bersad on 4 August. The next day the unit received word that a multi-engined Soviet aircraft had landed in the nearby village of Podvysokoye. It was possible that its crew had orders to rescue high-ranking officers or commissars of the surrounded Soviet army in the Uman pocket. Six CR.42s of the the 1/3. *vadászszázad* quickly took off, with százados Tomor leading the first section and hadnagy János Pettendi the second. Another pilot who took part in this mission was szakaszvezetö Lajos Göcsei.

They circled the village at 6000 ft but failed to locate the target. Tomor then spotted a building that looked like a command post and decided to investigate. He dived steeply, followed by the others. The anti-aircraft batteries remained silent, reluctant to betray their location too soon.

As his Fiat zoomed down, Tomor suddenly sighted a well-camouflaged three-engined machine standing next to a house on the outskirts of the village. Carefully aiming his fighter, he pressed the gun button, at which point the flak batteries opened up. But it was too late, for Tomor's tracers found their mark and the transport aircraft went up in flames. The remaining CR.42s sent at least one long burst into the burning aircraft.

The anti-aircraft fire was heavy and all of the fighters took hits. Indeed, only two were able to return to base. Two pilots were missing, but Göcsei soon telephoned to report that his aileron cable had been damaged and he had been forced to make an emergency landing at Anapol, 50 miles from Rovno. There was no news of Pettendi, however. Despite the ensuing aerial search, and inquiries pursued through intelligence channels, no trace of him was ever found. Pettendi had therefore become the squadron's first, and only, pilot to be killed in combat during this initial tour of duty in the east.

A few more sorties were flown before the unit moved to Pervomaysk on 9 August. At 0430 hrs on the 11th five Ca.135bis took off for a successful raid on Nikolayev. They also attacked a strategic bridge close to the city over the River Bug. The bombers were joined by an unusually strong fighter escort comprising six CR.42s of the 1/3. *vadászszázad* and five Re.2000s of the 1/2. *vadászszázad* over Pervomaysk airfield. Százados Tomor was the fighter leader. The Capronis flew out over the Black Sea east of Odessa, before making a wide circle to surprise the city's defences by coming in from the southeast. The leading aircraft released its bomb load on the central railway station from 1000 ft, while the other element of bombers attacked the bridge.

During their return flight the bombers were intercepted by nine Soviet I-16s. The six Hungarian fighters had been flying above the bombers as they left the target area, and they immediately engaged the *Ratas*, as did a handful of Re.2000s. When the Russian leader selected the first Caproni, he was in turn targeted by szakaszvezetö Lajos Göcsei and hadnagy Albert Seres. A turning dogfight followed, but the CR.42 pilots stayed behind the desperate Russian until Göcsei found himself in a favourable firing position. He sent a long burst into the I-16's fuselage, and flames erupted from the aircraft as it fell towards the ground.

Meanwhile, zászlós Miklós Kun had claimed another I-16 that had flown in front of his guns. When Tomor rejoined the bombers he discovered a lone I-16 behind one of the Capronis. He dived on the enemy and shot it down in flames. At the same time, zászlós Márton Szönyi and Baranyai, who were escorting a crippled Caproni, encountered two I-16s and promptly shot them down too. Seres, who had flown back in search of his squadronmates and a lone Ca.135bis, saw the two Soviet fighters crash.

These were the first five claims made by the 1/3. *vadászszázad* during World War 2. All the CR.42s had in turn been hit, but none was lost. The claimants were the squadron CO, százados Tomor, zászlós Kun, Szönyi and Baranyai and szakaszvezetö Göcsei (the latter shared his claim with hadnagy Seres). However, Re.2000 V.420 of föhadnagy Lasztóczy was missing, having possibly been shot down by flak. This was the 1/2. *vadászszázad's* first combat loss. The Soviet 9 IAP-ChF claimed three enemy aircraft shot down near Nikolayev, but two of its pilots, squadron

On 11 August 1941 the 1/3. *'Kör ász' vadászszázad* escorted Ca135bis bombers sent to attack Nikolayev. Over the target, the six escorting CR.42s were engaged by I-16s, and their pilots claimed five victories (one by százados László Tomor) without losses to them or to the bombers. Tomor is seen here sat on the tail of his CR.42, which displays a victory symbol. Tomor was decorated with the Hungarian *Signum Laudis* and the German *Eisernes Kreuz 1. und 2. Klasse* after his squadron's success (*Csaba Becze Archive*)

CO Kapitan Kolobkov and Leytenant Danchenko, were killed in air combat in the Nikolayev area.

A flight of CR.42s from the 1/3. *vadászszázad* advanced to the newly-captured Voznesensk airfield on 12 August, while six other fighters stayed put. Seven days later the 1/3. *vadászszázad* moved to Krivoy Rog. The unit flew several sorties over the industrial centre of Dniepropetrovsk during the following week. The first action came on 26 August, when hadnagy Albert Seres' section flew a sortie over the city and was engaged in combat by I-16s. Seres and zászlós Szönyi claimed two I-16s each, while zászlós Baranyai was credited with a fifth I-16. Baranyai's aircraft was damaged during this combat, and although he too was wounded, he managed to bring the fighter back. Baranyai received medical attention and flew again the next day. It is likely that the Hungarian pilots had been in combat with 88 IAP, which misidentified its opponents as 'Ar 197s'. The Soviet pilots claimed one victory.

The next day, föhadnagy Ujszászy's section was first over Dniepropetrovsk, where it surprised Soviet fighters taking off. During the combat, Ujszászy and törzsörmester Szobránci claimed two 'I-17s' (probably LaGG-3s or MiG-3s) each, while zászlós Ferenc Szénási was credited with a fifth. That evening, German intelligence confirmed the destruction of at least five aircraft. During a second patrol over Dniepropetrovsk, hadnagy Seres and zászlós Baranyai claimed two I-16s, although Zászlós Szönyi was rammed by Starshiy Leytenant Maltsev of 88 IAP and taken prisoner. It is possible that he had achieved a victory before he was downed, but there are no witnesses to support the claim. Maltsev managed to land his damaged I-16.

On 2 September százados Tomor and eight other pilots successfully strafed Soviet ground forces – this mission was repeated three days later. Over the next 12 days, six bomber escort missions were also flown.

Százados Tomor led five fighters to help an encircled German regiment east of Nikopol on 20 September, and on 10 October the *vadászszázad* moved to Dniepropetrovsk. One section was transferred to Golubovka and the other to Losovaya. However, the front moved so rapidly eastwards that it was not possible to fly sorties from these bases, so on 3 November the fighter, bomber and reconnaissance units, as well as the mobile workshop, were ordered to assemble at Dnieprodshershinsk. A few more missions were flown, and on 15 November the unit was told to prepare for its return to Hungary – the CR.42s, along with the Ju 86s and He 46s flown by the MKHL on the Eastern Front, were not considered suitable for the Russian winter. Indeed, no Hungarian combat aircraft saw service in Russia between December 1941 and May 1942.

On 18 November the 1/3. *vadászszázad* left the front, but the pilots were forced to land at Vinnitsa due to bad weather. They were grounded here for eight days, and it was not until the 26th that the unit crossed the Carpathians and set course for its home base at Mátyásföld.

During its time in the frontline, the 1/3. *vadászszázad* had claimed 17 victories and one probable during 114 missions and 447 individual combat sorties. Two pilots and two aircraft had been lost, with hadnagy Pettendi being killed and zászlós Szönyi captured.

A few CR.42s served with home-based fighter units until 1942, but they were eventually removed from frontline service and used as advanced

Sándor Szoják served in the 1/1. *'Íjász' vadászszázad's* 2. Section, flying CR.32s during the border skirmishes with the Slovaks in the spring of 1939. On 24 March he claimed two B.534s destroyed, the first of these falling in the Szobránc area. In 1940, Szojak changed his last name to Szobránci in honour of this claim. He would be credited with two and one shared victories in the CR.42 in 1941 (*Csaba Becze Archive*)

trainers. There were plans to employ some as nightfighters, but they were deemed unsuitable for this role because they lacked radios. In early 1944 a ground attack squadron was formed with the surviving CR.42s, bomb racks being installed under the wings of the aircraft. The squadron never saw active service, however.

Törzsormester Sándor Szobránci of the 1/3. *'Kör ász' vadászszázad* poses with his CR.42 and two mechanics. On 27 August 1941, Szobránci claimed two 'I-17s' (LaGG-3s or MiG-3s) over Uljanovka when the 1/3. *vadászszázad* was credited with five victories and one probable. These were Szobránci's last successes, taking his tally to 4 and 1 shared kills. After his tour with the 1/3. *vadászszázad* on the Eastern Front, he was awarded the *Nagy Ezüst Vitézségi Érem* (Great Silver Medal For Bravery). In the spring of 1945 Szobránci served in a Hungarian nightfighter unit, and soon after the war he emigrated to Australia (*Csaba Becze Archive*)

— Swedish J11s —

During the Finnish-Soviet Winter War that raged during early 1940, the Swedish volunteer unit F 19 (F standing for *Flygflottilj* or wing) served alongside its Scandanavian neighbours in defence of the northern part of the country against Soviet bomber raids. Although F 19 enjoyed some success, in order for it to be more effective the unit needed more modern fighters than the Gladiators it was equipped with.

In February 1940, a collection commenced in Sweden to raise funds for new fighters, this public aid for Finland being spurred on by a sermon preached by cleric Isaac Been, who declared 'What Finland really needs are fighters. And the devil shall be expelled by fighters'!

On 15 February an initial contract for five CR.42s was signed, followed on the 24th by a second for seven more. The type was selected mainly because of its immediate availability, and the ease with which skis could be fitted to its fixed undercarriage to permit operation from snow-covered airfields. It was intended that the CR.42s would enter service with F 19 in early April 1940, but with the end of the Winter War on 13 March, Finland declined to take delivery of the *Falcos*, preferring to receive the equivalent value in cash instead. The Royal Swedish Air Force (*Flygvapnet*) decided to take possession of the 12 fighters instead, using them as reconnaissance aircraft with F 3 at Linköping.

Sweden had also ordered fighters from the USA, but in mid-1940 the Americans decided to embargo the delivery of the 264 aircraft that the country had on order. The fighters affected by this delivery ban were the Seversky-Republic EP-1-106 (Swedish designation J9, J standing for *jaktplan* or fighter) and the Vultee Vanguard (J10), which were scheduled to equip F 8, F 9 and F 10. Only 60 had been delivered, however, when the embargo came into force. The Swedes urgently need new equipment, so the *Flygvapnet* decided to order an additional 60 CR.42s from Italy – in total, some 72 *Falcos* were ordered with the Swedish designation J11.

The CR.42s were delivered between April 1940 and September 1941, with all J11s being transferred to F 9 at Säve, in Gothenburg, as

F 9's '14' is seen in winter camouflage at Kiruna. Note the fighter's ski arrangement. These were used even after the J11s had been struck off charge, being fitted to Sk16 Texans. This particular *Falco* (2522) was delivered on 8 April 1941 and written off in a fatal accident on 20 February 1942. It had logged just 112 hours of flying time by then (*Mikael Forslund*)

replacements for the J9s that had not arrived from the US. By early 1942 two J11s were on permanent standby alert and one full division of the *Flygflottilj* was on 24-hour standby. From mid-March to late April 1942, 1.*divisionen* was based at Kiruna, in northern Sweden, to defend the ore-carrying rail link into Norway. At this time the aircraft were fitted with skis.

2. and 3.*divisionerna* remained at Säve, however, from where they attempted to perform a few interceptions over Swedish territory in order to escort intruders out of the country's airspace. The aircraft generally proved too slow to intercept either Allied or Axis machines, however. Despite this, the J11s were well liked by their pilots, although poor build quality and hard use resulted in many accidents, and they soon had to be replaced. In October 1943 F 9 started to exchange its J11s for the indigenous J22, allowing some of its *Falcos* to be transferred to the newly formed F 13. The remaining CR.42s were declared obsolete on 14 March 1945, and 13 aircraft (with six additional spare airframes) were purchased by *AB Svensk Flygtjänst* for use as target-tugs. In 1946 they were replaced by Miles Martinets. Only two CR.42s were retained as reserve aircraft, being flown sporadically until 1949.

GERMAN *FALCOS*

The German *Rüstungs-und-Kriegsproduktion Stab* ordered 200 CR.42LW (LW for Luftwaffe) aircraft in early 1943 to be used in the night harassment and anti-partisan roles. The aircraft were equipped with exhaust flame dampers, a pair of 12.7 mm machine guns and underwing racks for four 50 kg bombs. The *Rüstungs-und-Kriegsproduktion Stab* took control of Italy's aircraft industry after the Italian armistice in September 1943, and an American air raid on the Fiat factory in Turin destroyed several completed and semi-completed aircraft on the production line. This attack resulted in the construction of only 150 CR.42LWs, of which 112 were accepted into service by the Luftwaffe.

F 9's 1.*divisionen* is seen lined up in warmer weather. The unit's red devil insignia is visible beneath the cockpit of the aircraft nearest to the camera. Swedish CR.42s were flown hard in all weather conditions, causing them to quickly wear out. They were also obsolete virtually from the moment they were delivered, with pilots soon discovering that they were incapable of intercepting aircraft intruding into Swedish airspace. In October 1943 3.*divisionen* started to receive new Swedish-built FFVS J22 fighters, and in the spring and autumn of 1944, 1 and 2.*divisionerna* converted to the J22 (*Mikael Forslund*)

Ten experienced crews of *Nachtschlactgruppe* (NSGr) 3 were withdrawn from the northern sector of the Eastern Front during October 1943 to form the nucleus of NSGr 9, the pilots converting onto the Ca.314, which had been selected for use against partisans in the Alps, Istria and Croatia. Formally constituted on 30 November, 1./NSGr 9 moved to Udine, in Italy, in December to test the Caproni's combat-worthiness, initially in daylight. In January 1944, the unit transferred to Caselle, in Turin, to attack guerrillas in the southern Alpine area. However, 1./NSGr 9 only succeeded in establishing the Ca.314's unsuitability for the role. On 28 January a second *staffel* was established, this time with CR.42LWs.

By early 1944 the Luftwaffe high command was becoming impatient with the time being taken to bring NSGr 9 to operational readiness and, at the beginning of February, the unit commander was replaced. Hauptmann Rupert Frost would duly lead the unit until war's end. The landings at Anzio-Nettuno on 22 January 1944 hastened NSGr 9's 'promotion' to frontline service, and trial CR.42 sorties were flown following deployment of six aircraft to Viterbo in March. Operations were confined to moonlit periods since the crews were inexperienced, the biplanes carried no radio navigational aids and long flights had to be made over mountainous terrain in order to reach Allied targets.

Sorties were flown against high-value objectives within the Allied beachhead, often in the face of very strong defences. Initially, losses were few, and the Fiat was felt to have proved itself operationally. The aircraft were also used against Anglo-American forces around Monte Cassino, but the biplane's days with NSGr 9 were numbered owing to supply problems and the loss of five aircraft in a raid on Rieti by P-47s on 21 April. The combat status of 2. *Staffel's* aircraft fluctuated between 're-equipping', 'operational' and 'training' during the April-June period. Its *Staffelkapitän*, Oberleutnant Rolf Martini, was killed when his CR.42 crashed at Caselle on 22 May during a mock combat with Fiat's test pilot Valentino Cus.

From late February 1944 the *Falcos* were replaced by Ju 87Ds, which initially equipped 1. *Staffel*, while 2. *Staffel* continued to use the biplanes well into June. On 31 May 1944, 2./NSGr. 9 reported an establishment of 18 CR.42s of which 15 were serviceable.

At 0015 hrs on the night of 1/2 June, Australian Beaufighter pilot Flg Off D W Rees and his radar operator Flg Off D C Bartlett from No 600 Sqn picked up a contact 4.5 miles south of Rome. It was losing height and changing course, and the crew lost the contact when it entered the Anzio AA zone. When they picked it up again, the target was heading north, and weaving. A 15-minute pursuit ensued, with the Beaufighter closing at an indicated 110-120 mph and the pilot having to lower the aircraft's wheels and

Kapten Swanlund stands in front of 1.*divisionen* F 9's red devil in 1943. This squadron insignia began to appear on CR.42s from early 1942. Initially, the devil had a black skull painted on its chest, but in order to achieve higher visibility the skull was subsequently painted white. The figure featured black trousers, shoes, cloak and trident, and usually appeared on the port side of the fuselage only (*Mikael Forslund*)

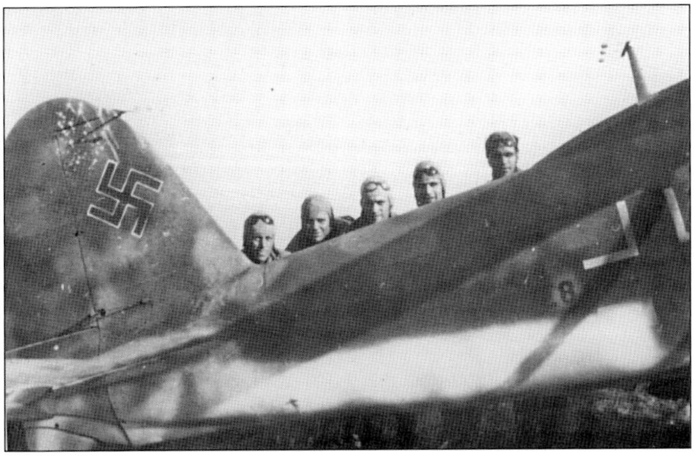

Pilots of 2./NSGr 9 are pictured 'taking cover' behind one of the *Staffel's* CR.42s in 1944. They are, from left to right, Unteroffizier Schmeiduch, Gefreiter Franz Spörr (killed in a flying accident on 28 November 1944), Gefreiter Ewald Kapahnke (killed in action on 3 July 1944), Feldwebel Horst Rau and Feldwebel Horst Greßler (wounded in action on 2 June 1944). Note the *Gruppe's* tiny 'E8' code, and the way the underside camouflage has partially covered by the *Balkenkreuz* (*Nick Beale*)

Feldwebel Horst Greßler and 'E8+BK' of 2./NSGr 9. Greßler was shot down and badly wounded over Lago di Vico following an attack on Anzio-Nettuno on the night of 1/2 June 1944. His was the first NSGr 9 machine to fall to an Allied nightfighter (Beaufighter MM905/M of No 600 Sqn, flown by Flg Offs Stewart W Rees (RAAF) and D C Bartlett). Horst Greßler returned to operations with NSGr 9 some months later. He also saw action in both the Ju 87D and Fw 190 (*Nick Beale*)

flaps in order to slow it down. Finally, the pursued aircraft was identified as a CR.42. The nightfighter closed in from down-moon and dead astern to a distance of just 50 yards, fired a short burst and 'blew the biplane up in a mass of flames' – the burning pieces were seen to fall into Lake Vico. The aircraft had been piloted by Feldwebel Gressler of 2./NSGr 9, who had been attacking Allied gun positions and columns in the Artena-Giulianello-Cori area southeast of Rome. He was injured when his CR.42 crashed at Fabrica di Roma.

On 2 June 2./NSGr 9's Ju 87s started to arrive, with 14 examples flying in from the Eastern Front. Six days later, NSGr 9 brought three CR.42s and a pair of Stukas to Bologna. With the arrival of the Ju 87s, the *Falcos* were phased out, the last known sorties with the type being flown in the middle of June.

The newly-formed 3./NSGr 7 at Zagreb, in Croatia, was equipped with CR.42LWs in April 1944. The *Gruppe's* other two *staffeln* operated a mix of elderly He 46s, Hs 126s and Do 17s on anti-partisan duties in the Balkans. By September, 2. *Staffel* had been transferred to Pleso, also in Croatia, from where it flew 26 CR.42LWs alongside 3. *Staffel*, which was already deployed there. The Fiats later equipped 1. *Staffel*, based at Graz, in Austria.

On 8 February 1945, ten CR.42s of *Stab* and 2. *Staffel* of NSGr 7 took off from their base at Agram-Gorica, in Croatia, on an anti-partisan mission. Their intended target was Grabovica airfield, which was used by partisan forces, but at the last moment the target area was changed and they were sent to attack partisans northwest of Sisak. Several miles southeast of Agram-Gorica, the CR.42 formation was jumped by P-38s of the 14th FG. During the ensuing battle, NSGr 7 lost four CR.42LWs – three fell to P-38s and one to groundfire.

According to US records, between 1216 hrs and 1232 hrs, 1Lt Lawrence Bach Jr of the 37th FS claimed to have shot down two biplanes, plus one probable and one damaged. However, research by historian Csaba Becze has shown that the battle was not all one-sided, as an NSGr 7 pilots claimed a P-38 destroyed during the same dogfight. The German pilot remains unidentified, however, and there is no mention of him in existing documentation. What is known is that the 14th FG did lose two P-38s during this mission, making this the last biplane combat victory ever claimed.

When World War 2 ended in Europe on 7 May 1945, more than 20 CR.42LWs remained operational with NSGr 7's *Gruppenstab* and 2. and 3. *Staffeln*, based at Zagreb-Goriza, as well as 1. *Staffel* at Graz. NSGr 20, based in France, also operated an unknown number of CR.42ASs, as did various Luftwaffe flight schools and training units, who used them as fighter-trainers. One such outfit was JG 107 at Toul. Trainee Luftwaffe pilots nicknamed the CR.42 *Die Pressluftorgel* (the pneumatic organ), presumably because of its profusion of pneumatic systems.

Designed and built at a time when most air forces were re-equipping with monoplanes, the Fiat CR.42 was obsolete by the time it entered frontline service in the late 1930s. Nevertheless, in the early months of the war at least, it was still able to prove itself a reasonably effective fighter, and one that, in the hands of a skilled and experienced pilot, could well shame more modern machinery.

APPENDICES

Regia Aeronautica CR.42 Aces

Name	CR.42 Score	Total Score	CR.42 Unit(s)	Notes
Mario Visintini	16+2sh/1/-	17+2sh/1/-	412ª *Sq*	Top biplane fighter ace of World War 2
Lugi Baron	12+2sh/-/-	12+2sh/-/-	412ª *Sq*	All victories in East Africa
Aroldo Soffritti	8/5/-	8/5/-	412ª *Sq*	All victories in East Africa
Carlo Canella	7/-/-	7/-/-	412ª *Sq*	All victories in East Africa
Giulio Torresi	6/-/1sh	10+10sh/5+2sh/11sh	77ª *Sq*	
Guglielmo Chiarini	5+8sh/-/-	5+8sh/-/-	82ª and 366ª *Sq*	
Giorgio Graffer	5+4sh/-/-	5+4sh/-/-	365ª *Sq*	One nocturnal claim
Leonardo Ferrulli	5+2sh/2sh/1	21+3sh/1+2sh/1	91ª *Sq*	
Franco Bordoni-Bisleri	5/-/-	19/4/-	95ª *Sq*	

Regia Aeronautica Aces with CR.42 claims

Name	CR.42 Score	Total Score	CR.42 Unit(s)	Notes
Paolo Arcangeletti	1/1/-	5/1/-	393ª *Sq*	At least one with CR.42
Giovanni Barcaro	1sh/-/-	9+4sh/-/-	97ª *Sq*	
Osvaldo Bartolozzi	2/-/-	6+1sh/-/-	413ª *Sq*	
Alessandro Bladelli	5sh/-/-1sh	5+7sh/1/5+1sh	91ª *Sq*	
Pietro Bonfatti	2+4sh/1+1sh/4sh	6+7sh/2+3sh/4sh	73ª *Sq*	
Ernesto Botto	3+3sh/-/1+4sh	8+20sh/-/1+4sh	9º *Gr*	
Francesco Cuscuna	1/1sh/2sh	5/1sh/2sh	75ª *Sq*	At least one with CR.42
Rinaldo Damiani	3sh/-/4sh	6+3sh/-/4sh	97ª *Sq*	
Ugo Drago	4+3sh/-/-	17+3sh/-/-	363ª *Sq*	
Domenico Facchini	1sh/-/1sh	5+1sh/1/1sh	365ª *Sq*	At least one shared with CR.42
Guido Fibbia	1/-/-	9/-/-	95ª *Sq*	At least one with CR.42
Luigi Filippi	1/-/-	7+1sh/-/-	75ª *Sq*	At least one with CR.42
Armando François	1/-/-	7/-/-	4º *St*	
Jacopo Frigerio	3sh/-/4sh	5+4sh/1/4sh	97ª *Sq*	
Antonia Giardinà	4+1sh/-/-	5+3sh/-/2	410ª and 412ª *Sq*	All victories in East Africa
Eber Giudice	2/-/-	5/-/-	393ª *Sq*	At least two with CR.42
Luigi Gorrini	2/-/-	19/-/9	85ª *Sq*	
Amedeo Guidi	3+1sh/1/1	6+1sh/1/1	366ª *Sq*	
Antonio Larsimont	1+4sh/-/7sh	7+5sh/1/1+7sh	97ª *Sq* and 9º *Gr*	
Felice Longhi	1+3sh/-/4sh	6+4sh/-/4sh	95ª *Sq*	
Franco Lucchini	3+15sh/2sh/3	22+52sh/2+2sh/6+3sh	90ª *Sq*	
Orlando Mandolini	1sh/-/1+1sh	7+1sh/-/1+1sh	93ª and 91ª *Sq*	At least one shared with CR.42
Luigi Mariotti	4sh/-/-	5+6sh/-/-	363ª *Sq*	At least four shared with CR.42

Teresio Martinoli	3/-/-	22+14sh/2+1sh/1+4sh	384ª, 78ª and 84ª *Sq*	
Alfonso Mattei	4sh/-/-	5+5sh/-/-	153ª *Sq*	
Fiorenzo Milella	1+1sh/1/1sh	5+1sh/1/1sh	366ª *Sq*	
Elio Miotto	7sh/2sh/-	5+7sh/2sh/-	91ª *Sq*	
Luigi Monti	0+18sh/2sh/1	8+18sh/2sh/1	84ª *Sq*	Claims with CR.42?
Giuseppe Mottet	1+1sh/-/2	6+4sh/-/2	411ª *Sq*	
Giuseppe Oblach	1/1/1	7/2/1	73ª *Sq*	
Enzo Omiccioli	4/-/-	5+2sh/-/-	412ª *Sq*	
Luciano Perdoni	2sh/2sh/-	5+3sh/2sh/-	84ª *Sq*	
Ranieri Piccolomini	1/-/3	7+12sh/4+3sh/4	92ª *Sq*	
Mario Pinna	1+1sh/-/-	5+4sh/1/1	70ª and 74ª *Sq*	At least one with CR.42
Alvaro Querci	2sh/-/-	6+5sh/1+1sh/3sh	73ª *Sq*	
Giulio Reiner	3+1sh/2+1sh/-	10+57sh/7+23sh/2+9sh	73ª *Sq*	
Vito Rinaldi	2/1/-	9+9sh/2/-	94ª and 301ª *Sq*	
Carlo Romagnoli	1+13sh/6sh/-	11+13sh/6sh/-	10º *Gr*	
Giuseppe Ruzzin	1+3sh/-/3sh	5+6sh/-/8+4sh	85ª *Sq*	
Massimo Salvatore	1/-/1	10+5sh/2/1	97ª *Sq*	At least one with CR.42
Angelo Savini	4sh/-/-	7+5sh/1+1sh/-	90ª *Sq*	
Giuseppe Scarpetta	1/-/-	6/-/-	395ª *Sq*	At least one with CR.42
Claudio Solaro	1+2sh/1/-	12+14/1/-	70ª *Sq*	
Giorgio Solaroli	1sh/-/-	11+5sh/7/-	74ª *Sq*	
Alberto Spigaglia	4sh/-/-	6+4sh/-/-	364ª *Sq*	At least four shared with CR.42
Luigi Torchio	1/-/-	5/-/-	377ª *Sq*	
Giorgio Tugnoli	1+4sh/-/-	6+4sh/1/-	153ª *Sq*	At least one with CR.42
Mario Veronesi	2+2sh/2sh/1	11+6sh/2+2sh/1	84ª *Sq*	
Ezio Viglione	1+4sh/-/1+4sh	5+6sh/-/1+4sh	97ª *Sq*	
Celso Zemella	1sh/-/-	5+1sh/-/-	70ª *Sq*	At least one with CR.42
Gianmario Zuccarini	1/1/1sh	5+3sh/1/1sh	77ª *Sq*	

Leading *Regia Aeronautica* non-Aces in the CR.42

Name	CR.42 Score	Total Score	CR.42 Unit(s)	Notes
Corrado Santoro	4/3/1	4/3/1	413ª and 370ª *Sq*	
Agostino Fausti	4/-/-	4/-/-	77ª *Sq*	
Guido Bobba	3+1sh/1/-	3+1sh/1/-	74ª *Sq*	
Osvaldo Bartolaccini	3/-/-	3/-/-	364ª *Sq*	At least three with CR.42
Mario Gaetano Carancini	3+3sh/-	3+3sh/-	393ª *Sq*	
Furio Lauri	2+1sh/-/-	2+1sh/-/-	368ª *Sq*	Once credited with 11 kills
Oscar Molinari	3/-/-	3/-/-	160º *Gr*	
Ernesto Pavan	3/-/-	4/-/-	92ª *Sq*	
Walter Ratticchieri	3/-/-	3/-/-	393ª *Sq*	
Maurizio Nicolis di Robilant	3+1sh/-/-	3+1sh/-/-	363ª *Sq*	
Bernardino Serafini	3/-/2	3/1sh/2	366ª *Sq*	
Luciano Tarantini	3+1sh/1/1	3+1sh/1/1	160º *Gr*	

Leading Belgian CR.42 pilots

Name	CR.42 Score	Total Score	CR.42 unit
Jean Offenberg	1/-/1	5+2sh/5/5+2sh	4/II/2 *Aé*
Jean de Callataÿ	2/-/-	2/-/-	3/II/2 *Aé*
Charles Goffin	2/-/1	2/-/1	3/II/2 *Aé*
Werner de Mérode	1/-/-	1/-/-	3/II/2 *Aé*
Alexis Jottard	-/-/1	-/-/1	4/II/2 *Aé*
Jan Maes	-/-/1	-/-/1	4/II/2 *Aé*
Marcel Michotte	-/-/1	-/-/1	4/II/2 *Aé*
Emile de Moerlose	-/-/1	-/-/1	4/II/2 *Aé*
Jean Moreau	-/-/1	-/-/1	4/II/2 *Aé*

Leading Hungarian CR.42 pilots

Name	CR.42 Score	Total Score	CR.42 unit
György Ujszászy	2+1sh/-/-	7+1sh/-/3	1/3. *vadászszázad*
László Pottyondy	1/1/-	13/1/-	2/3. *vadászszázad*
Sándor Szobránci (Szojak)	2+1sh/-/-	4+1sh/-/-	1/3. *vadászszázad*
Márton Szönyi	4(?)/-/-	4(?)/-/-	1/3. *vadászszázad*
Károly Baranyai	3/-/-	3/-/-	1/3. *vadászszázad*
Albert Seres	3/-/-	3/-/-	1/3. *vadászszázad*
Aladár Szobránczy (Negró)	1/-/-	3/-/-	2/3. *vadászszázad*
Árpád Kertész	1/-/-	2/-/1	2/3. *vadászszázad*
Gyözö Vámos	2/-/1sh	2/-/1sh	2/3. *vadászszázad*
János Balogh	1/-/-	1/-/-	2/3. *vadászszázad*
Lajos Göcsei	1/-/-	1/-/-	1/3. *vadászszázad*
Miklós Kun	1/-/-	1/-/-	1/3. *vadászszázad*
Péter Soós	1/-/-	1/-/-	2/3. *vadászszázad*
Ferenc Szénási	1+1sh/-/-	1+1sh/-/-	1/3. *vadászszázad*
László Tomor	1/-/-	1/-/-	1/3. *vadászszázad*

Note

Scores split as follows – destroyed/probably destroyed/damaged

All drawings on this spread are of a Fiat CR.42 *Falco*, and they are to 1/48th scale

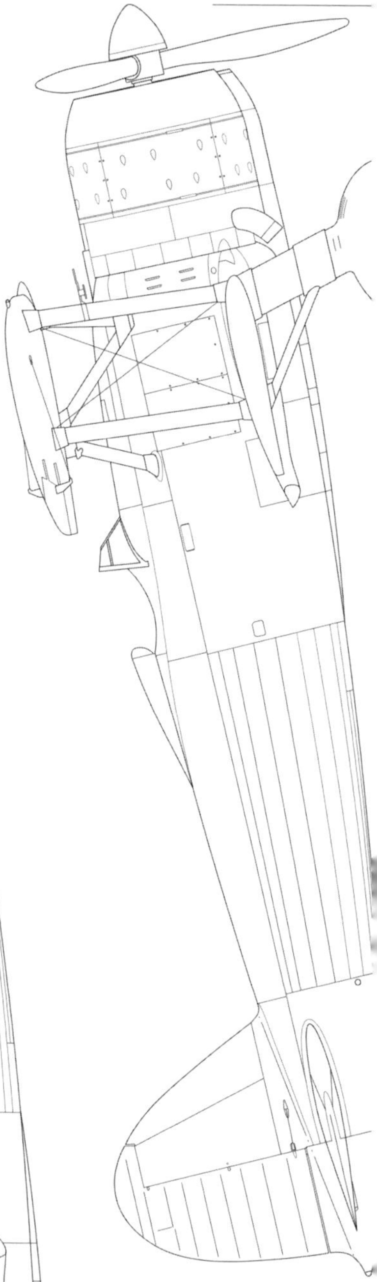

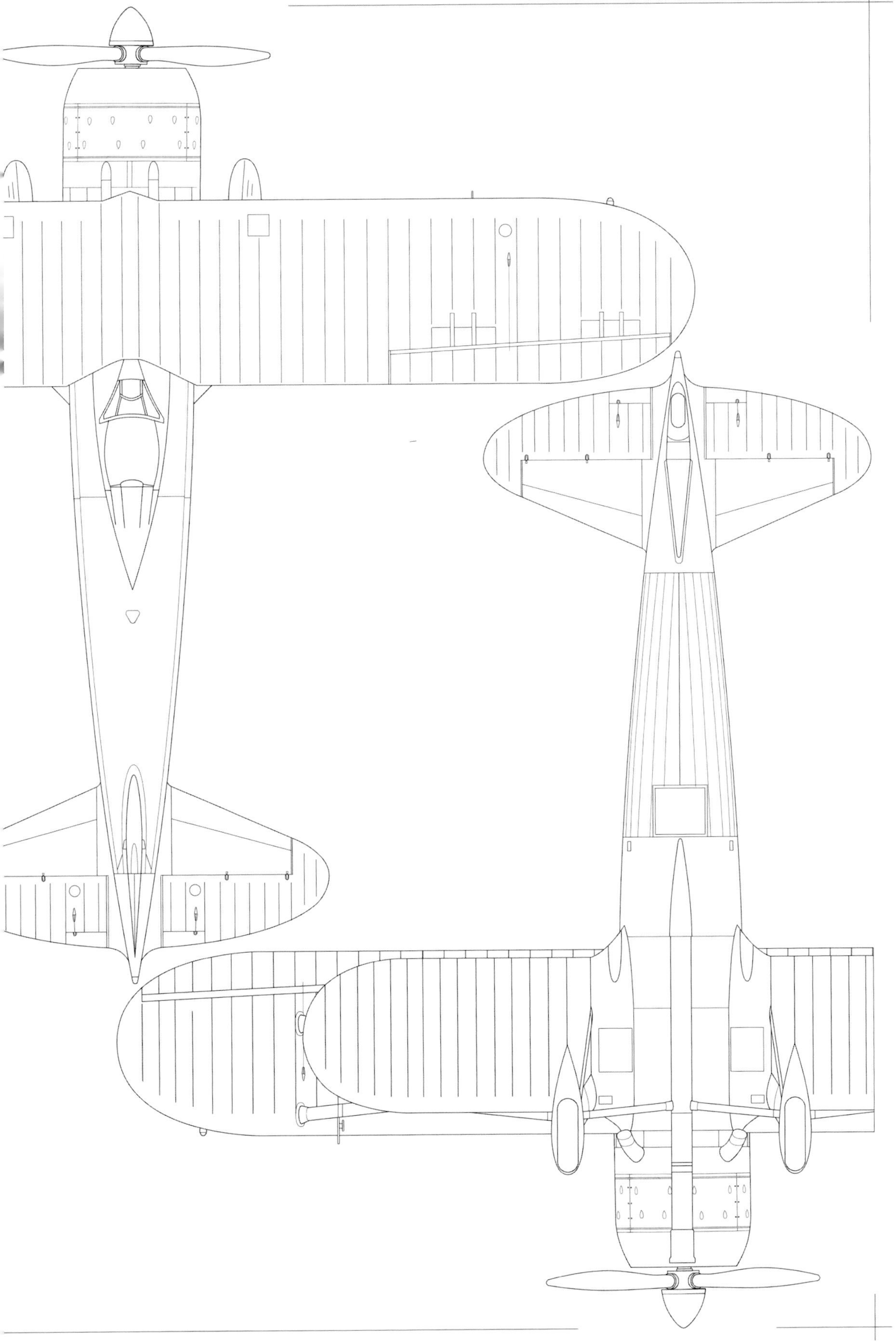

COLOUR PLATES

1

CR.42 MM4393 of Maggiore Ernesto Botto, CO of 9° *Gruppo*, 4° *Stormo*, Benina, summer 1940

Botto was an ace from the Spanish Civil War, having claimed five victories in the CR.32 prior to being wounded and losing a leg. He was to claim three additional kills with the CR.42. This aircraft displays the prancing horse insignia of 9° *Gruppo* (white horse on black shield) and the red lightning bolt of 73ª *Squadriglia* on its wheel spats, as well as the *Gruppo* CO's pennant on the fuselage.

2

CR.42CN MM7584 of Capitano Corrado Ricci, CO of 300ª *Squadriglia*, 167° *Gruppo Autonomo*, Ciampino, spring 1942

Ricci was also a Spanish Civil War veteran, having claimed five victories in that conflict. He served in the East African campaign prior to forming and commanding the first specialised nightfighter unit in the *Regia Aeronautica*, 300ª *Squadriglia*. This unit was based at Ciampino and tasked with the night defence of Rome between January and May 1942, although it made no interceptions during this time. MM7584 is equipped with a searchlight beneath its port wing.

3

CR.42CN of Capitano Luciano Marcolin, CO of 377ª *Squadriglia Autonoma*, Palermo-Boccadifalco, autumn 1942

Tasked with defending the night skies of Sicily, 377ª *Squadriglia* was based at Palermo-Boccadifalco in 1942-43. A section of CR.42CNs was attached to the unit in September 1942 for nightfighter and anti-submarine duties. The squadron CO during this period was Luciano Marcolin, who had also seen action in the Spanish Civil War.

4

CR.42 (serial unknown) of 77ª *Squadriglia*, 13° *Gruppo*, 2° *Stormo*, Castelbenito, summer 1940

This aircraft displays 77ª *Squadriglia's* 'ace of hearts' war badge on the wheel fairing, as well as the special insignia of a red star inside an azure blue rectangular flag to indicate that this is the personal machine of a Generale di Brigata Aerea. There is a strong possibility that this fighter was flown by Generale Guglielmo Cassinelli, CO of *Brigata Aerea Rex*.

5

CR.42 MM5649 of 96ª *Squadriglia*, 9° *Gruppo*, 4° *Stormo*, El Adem, autumn 1940

This aircraft is painted in the standard three-tone camouflage scheme of the period, and it displays the prancing horse insignia of 9° *Gruppo*, together with an additional 'Iron leg' badge on the fin. It also carries the white flash on the wheel spats commonly seen on aircraft assigned to 96ª *Squadriglia*.

6

CR.42 (serial unknown) of Sergente Maggiore Sante Morandi, 413ª *Squadriglia Autonoma*, Somaliland, August 1940

413ª *Squadriglia* served with distinction in the central and northern fronts of Italian East Africa. Although carrying the personal number '1', this fighter was not the personal machine of the *squadriglia* CO. It has been painted in a standard three-tone camouflage scheme, and is known to have been flown by Sergente Maggiore Sante Morandi.

7

CR.42 MM5701 of Sergente Pietro Salvadori, 95ª *Squadriglia*, 18° *Gruppo*, 56° *Stormo*, Ursel, 11 November 1940

Salvadori was a member of the *CAI*, he force-landed with engine trouble on a beach near the Orfordness lighthouse on 11 November 1940. His aircraft was made serviceable by the RAF and flown in evaluation trails as BT474. It has been an exhibit in the Battle of Britain Museum at RAF Hendon for more than 20 years.

8

CR.42 MM4387 of 77ª *Squadriglia*, 13° *Gruppo*, 2° *Stormo*, Castelbenito, summer 1940

When Italy declared war on Britain and France in June 1940, 13° *Gruppo* was the only fighter unit in Libya equipped with CR.42s. 77ª *Squadriglia* claimed its first victories on 29 June when pilots reported shooting down five aircraft during an engagement with No 113 Sqn, which lost three Blenheim Is. The *squadriglia's* 'ace of hearts' badge was the personal insignia of World War 1 ace Pier Ruggero Piccio.

9

CR.42 (serial unknown) of Capitano Guido Bobba, 74ª *Squadriglia*, 23° *Gruppo Autonomo*, Turin-Mirafiori, July 1940

This is a speculative illustration based on the personal number '1' carried on the machine. This number was very often applied to the aircraft assigned to the *Squadriglia's* commanding officer. Bobba served as CO of 74ª *Squadriglia*, and claimed three victories with the CR.42 over Malta between July and November 1940. The red-white-green spinner was distinctive to this *squadriglia*, as was the unofficial badge seen on the fin of this aircraft, depicting a black hawk inside a red circle. This was inspired by the name of the aircraft (*Falco*) and the *gruppo* leader (Falconi).

10

CR.42 (serial unknown) of Sottotenente Franco Bordoni-Bisleri, 95ª *Squadriglia*, 18° *Gruppo*, 3° *Stormo*, Mirafiori, summer 1940

This profile reveals a rare example of individualisation displayed on an Italian aircraft, Sottotenente Bordoni-Bisleri having his nickname, *ROBUR*, painted on the headrest of his CR.42. Bordoni-Bisleri belonged to a family of industrialists who produced what was at the time a popular Italian digestive liquor (*'Ferro-China Bisleri'*). The badge shown on the bottles was of a lion with the word 'Robur' ('strength' in Latin), and this was also Bordoni-Bisleri's nickname, which he had painted on most of his aircraft. Bordoni-Bisleri claimed five victories with the CR.42 in 1941.

11

CR.42 (serial unknown) of Tenente Edoardo Crainz, 394ª *Squadriglia,* 160° *Gruppo Autonomo,* Koritza, December 1940

This aircraft sustained damage in combat on 21 December 1940 when Crainz claimed two No 80 Sqn Gladiators destroyed over Argyrokastron. His mechanics covered the bullet holes in the fighter's rear fuselage with small tricolour patches – a tradition that stretched back to World War 1. On the fuselage side just forward of the cockpit can be seen the silhouette of Mussolini's head. This was an unofficial *squadriglia* marking that was adopted by 394ª during the Greek campaign.

12

CR.42 (serial unknown) of Maggiore Tito Falconi, CO of 23° *Gruppo Autonomo,* Trapani-Milo, June 1940

This aircraft displays a slanting white band on the fuselage, indicating its assignment to the *gruppo* leader. The extended cross on the tail was not unusual for this unit either. Tito Falconi claimed one victory while flying the CR.42 when, on 7 September 1940, he was credited with downing a Hurricane over Valetta, Malta.

13

CR.42 (serial unknown) of Sergente Maggiore Luigi Baron, 412ª *Squadriglia Autonoma,* Asmara, early 1941

Luigi Baron claimed 12 victories with the CR.42 over East Africa and was the second most successful pilot of this campaign. His scoring streak was eventually brought to an end by No 1 Sqn SAAF Hurricanes on 25 March 1941 when he was shot in the thigh dogfighting with Hurricanes from No 1 Squadron SAAF. Baron spent more than two years in hospital recovering from his wounds before being repatriated. This machine displays no individual markings, as there was little time for the application of unit insignia, or other tactical emblems, on reinforcement fighters newly arrived from Italy at the beginning of 1941, prior to them being rushed to the frontline.

14

CR.42 (serial unknown) of Tenente Mario Visintini, 412ª *Squadriglia Autonoma,* Barentu, late 1940

Mario Visintini was the top-scoring biplane ace of World War 2. A veteran of the Spanish Civil War, where he claimed one victory in the CR.32, he was officially credited with 16 and two shared kills with the CR.42 in East Africa prior to his death in a flying accident on 11 February 1941. No illustrations of his fighter exist, and the tactical marking '412-2' applied to the aircraft in this profile is speculative. The 412ª *Squadriglia* emblem (a red prancing horse over a black silhouette of Africa) is, however, shown in at least one photograph of a unit aircraft (see page 44).

15

CR.42 MM4382 of Tenente Mario Rigatti, 75ª *Squadriglia,* 23° *Gruppo Autonomo,* Comiso, August 1940

On 24 August 1940 Mario Rigatti claimed to have shot down a No 261 Sqn Hurricane over Malta before being hit and returning to Comiso with serious wounds. This was Rigatti's only individual victory in the CR.42. In a situation reminiscent of Botto's story, Rigatti subsequently learned how to fly again, despite being fitted with an artificial leg. He rejoined his unit at the end of 1942.

16

CR.42 (serial unknown) Colonnello Raffraele Colacicchi, CO of 15° *Stormo d'Assalto,* Cyrenaica, October 1942

Raffaele Colacicchi was a well-known test pilot in the 1930s, and in 1942 he commanded 15° *Stormo d'Assalto.* This *Falco* displays a *stormo* badge on the fin in the form of a flying duck wearing iron pants and throwing bombs from its wings. The *stormo's* number on the fuselage and the rank stripes on the wheel spats were peculiar to this particular machine. 15° *Stormo* was widely employed in the ground attack role in North Africa from September 1942 through to February 1943, and it suffered heavy losses during this period.

17

CR.42 MM7117 of Sottotenente Ildebrando Malavolta, 110° *Squadriglia Autonoma,* Gondar, October 1941

This aircraft was the last CR.42 to be lost in combat in East Africa. On 24 October 1941, Malavolta was ordered to fly an urgent reconnaissance mission in the only serviceable aircraft then available in-theatre, MM7117. He was duly shot down and killed in the Ambazzo area by Lt L C H Hope of No 3 Sqn SAAF, who was flying a Gladiator. The fighter displays the black diagonal cross on a white field that was a tactical marking applied to all Italian aircraft late on in the East African campaign.

18

CR.42 (serial unknown) of Colonello Arrigo Tessari, CO of 53° *Stormo,* Turin, 10 October 1940

Colonello Tessari commanded 53° *Stormo* during the early months of the war, and he led this unit during the attacks on southern France in mid-1940. Indeed, he claimed four shared victories on 15 June during the widespread attacks on French airfields in Provence. This aircraft displays a *stormo* command pennant and a diagonal white stripe on the rear fuselage/tail for in-flight identification.

19

CR.42 (serial unknown) of Capitano Giorgio Graffer, 365ª *Squadriglia,* 150° *Gruppo Autonomo,* Argyrokastron, November 1940

CR.42 ace Giorgio Graffer was well known as a mountaineer pre-war. Seeing plenty of action between August and November 1940, he claimed a Whitley shot down during a night interception over Turin and four victories over Greece, prior to being killed in combat with No 80 Sqn Gladiators on 28 November 1940. Graffer was posthumously awarded a *Medaglia d'oro al valor militare.*

20

CR.42 MM4462 of Maggiore Ferruccio Vosilla, CO of 18° *Gruppo,* Turin-Mirafiori, October 1940

Maggiore Ferruccio Vosilla led 18° *Gruppo* during the attacks on southern France in June 1940, as well as during the unit's unsuccessful attacks on England five months later. This CR.42 displays a *gruppo* command pennant under the cockpit and a non-standard white band on the rear fuselage.

21

CR.42 (serial unknown) of Sergente Luigi Gorrini, 85ª *Squadriglia,* 18° *Gruppo,* 3° *Stormo,* Villanova D'Albenga, June 1940

Luigi Gorrini also took part in operations over France and southern England as part of the *CAI* in 1940. He claimed his first two victories with the CR.42 over North Africa in 1941 and ended the war with 19 victories to his name. The remainder were claimed while flying the Macchi C.202 and C.205V. Following its operations against France, this particular fighter was sent to reinforce units based in North Africa.

22

CR.42 MM4304 of Capitano Corrado Santoro, 413ª *Squadriglia Autonoma,* Diredawa, August 1940

Corrado Santoro shot down Blenheim I L8474 of No 39 Sqn and badly damaged a second bomber from No 11 Sqn over Diredawa on 20 August 1940. After returning from the *AOI,* he claimed three more victories on 27 September 1941 while flying the CR.42. He continued to serve in the Italian air force post-war, and ended his career as a Generale di Divisione Aerea.

23

CR.42 MM4308 of Tenente Enzo Martissa, 91ª *Squadriglia,* 10° *Gruppo,* 4° *Stormo,* El Adem, August 1940

Enzo Martissa force-landed on 8 August 1940 after combat with No 80 Sqn Gladiators. This fighter displays the black griffin insignia on its wheel spat that had been the badge of 91ª *Squadriglia* since World War 1.

24

CR.42 of Tenente Colonello Rolando Pratelli, CO of 150° *Gruppo,* Valona, March 1941

Tenente Colonello Rolando Pratelli commanded 53° *Stormo* when the war commenced, leading it during the airfield attacks on southern France in June 1940. Like Colonello Tessari of 53° *Stormo,* Pratelli also claimed four shared victories during the attack on airfields in Provence on 15 June. Strangely, this machine displays a *stormo* command pennant, despite Pratelli, who was already a tenente colonello, still being a *gruppo* CO at the time. The CR.42 also has a diagonal white ribbon on the rear fuselage/tail for identification.

25

CR.42 MM5024 of Capitano Aldo Li Greci, CO of 385ª *Squadriglia,* 157° *Gruppo,* 1° *Stormo,* Trapani-Milo, July 1940

385ª *Squadriglia* escorted bombers attacking airfields in the Tunis area on 13 June 1940, and the unit's pilots claimed one aerial victory without any combat loss to themselves or to the bombers they were escorting. This aircraft was personalised with a white lightning bolt insignia that does not appear to have been an officially recognised unit badge.

26

CR.42 (serial unknown) of Capitano Virginio Teucci, CO of 375ª *Squadriglia,* 160° *Gruppo,* Brindisi, June 1941

Formed in Albania on 1 February 1941, 375ª *Squadriglia* completed the establishment of 160° *Gruppo,* which until then had numbered only two *squadriglie.* Capitano Virgino Teucci of 2° *Stormo* was its leader, and his fighter is depicted here as it appeared during the unit's return to Treviso from Albania at the end of the Greek campaign. The CR.42 displays the *squadriglia* CO's triangular pennant on its side.

27

CR.42 (serial unknown) of 368ª *Squadriglia,* 151° *Gruppo,* Mellaha, April 1941

One of the units that most distinguished itself during the first Libyan campaign up to February 1941, 368ª *Squadriglia* was to remain in-theatre until the summer, during which time it was mainly employed on convoy escort missions and point defence duty. The white circle on the wheel fairing has been documented as appearing on aircraft from both *368ª* and *366ª Squadriglie,* and it possibly served as a *gruppo* identification marking.

28

CR.42 R.5 of 4/II/1 *Aé,* Nivelles, May 1940

This CR.42 of 4/II/1 *Aé* displays the *Escadrille's* badge in the form of a white *cocotte* (paper duck) as used by ranking Belgian ace Willy Coppens during World War 1. When the German assault in the west was launched on 10 May 1940, R.5 was on the unit's strength, but it was caught up in the events following the attack and its final fate is unknown.

29

CR.42 R.17 of 3/II/1 *Aé,* Brustem, 10 May 1940

This CR.42 of 3/II/1 *Aé* displays the *Escadrille's* red *cocotte* insignia. It did not see combat and was destroyed at Brustem on 10 May when Ju 87Bs from I./StG 2 attacked and destroyed 14 CR.42s on the ground, effectively wiping out 3/II/1 *Aé.*

30

CR.42 R.21 of 4/II/1 *Aé,* Nivelles, May 1940

This CR.42 of 4/II/1 *Aé* was unserviceable on 10 May, which meant that it had to be left behind at Nivelles when the unit hastily redeployed to Brustem. The fighter was damaged in an attack by Ju 87s from 4./StG 2 on Nivelles that same day, being destroyed inside one of the bombed-out hangars at the airfield.

31

CR.42 R.30 of 1Sgt Marcel Michotte, 4/II/1 *Aé,* Brustem, 10 May 1940

This aircraft was nosed over by Michotte when he landed on what was for him the unknown Landing Field No 22 at Brustem following the evacuation of Nivelles in the early morning hours of 10 May. Although the aircraft was not badly damaged, it was caught up in the lightning invasion of Belgium by German forces and never repaired.

32

CR.42 V.203 of the 1/3. *'Kör Ász' vadászszázad,* Mátyásföld, early autumn 1939

The factory-fresh silver V.203 as it looked when it arrived in Hungary during the autumn of 1939. 1/3. *'Kör Ász' vadászszázad* was the first Hungarian unit to be equipped with CR.42s.

33

CR.42 V.203 of the 1/3. *'Kör Ász' vadászszázad*, Mátyásföld, 1939-40

This aircraft was used by zászlós Márton Szönyi on 26 August 1941 when he claimed to have shot down two Russian I-16s. This profile is, however, based on the aircraft's appearance during the 1939-40 period, since the 1/3. *'Kör Ász' vadászszázad's* insignia was changed during 1940 to a simpler form without the disc. The fighter also wears the old three-tone camouflage scheme initially applied to the CR.42s in 1939. From April 1941 yellow bands were painted on the fuselage behind the cockpit.

34

CR.42 V.206 of százados László Tomor, the 1/3. *'Kör Ász' vadászszázad*, Pervomaysk, August 1941

Százados László Tomor claimed to have shot down an I-16 in the Nikolayev area on 11 August 1941 while the unit was escorting Ca.135bis bombers attacking Nikolayev. The 1/3. *vadászszázad* was credited with five victories without any losses during this mission. V.206 had been damaged during a strafing mission on 22 July and the bullet holes covered over with fabric patches decorated with red stars.

35

CR.42 V.234 of the 5/1. *'Kör Ász' vadászszázad*, Matyasföld, April 1942

V.234 displays the new national marking introduced during 1942. When the 1/3. *'Kör Ász' vadászszázad* returned from the Eastern Front it was re-designated the 5/1. *'Kör Ász' vadászszázad*.

36

CR.42 V.267 of föhadnagy László Kázár, 2/3. *'Ricsi' vadászszázad*, Eastern Front, late summer 1941

Föhadnagy László Kázár's CR.42 V.267 was shot up in combat during the late summer of 1941. The holes were covered over with fabric patches marked with white stars. Kázár later claimed two victories on the Eastern Front during 1942.

37

CR.42LW (serial unknown) of Feldwebel Horst Greßler of 2./NSGr. 9, Viterbo, spring 1944

Greßler was shot down and badly wounded over Lago di Vico following an attack on Anzio-Nettuno on the night of 1/2 June 1944. His was the first NSGr 9 machine to fall to an Allied nightfighter – in this case Beaufighter MM905/M of No 600 Sqn, flown by Flg Offs Stewart W Rees (RAAF) and D C Bartlett. Horst Greßler returned to operations with NSGr 9 in late 1944, flying Ju 87Ds and Fw 190s before war's end.

38

CR.42 2522 (construction number 780) of F 9's 1.*divisionen*, Kiruna, 1941

CR.42 2522 is illustrated here with wheel spats still in place after skis had been installed – a practice that was abandoned after several years. This aircraft was destroyed on 20 February 1942 during a practice combat when Furir Allan Turneryd lost control of his fighter at low altitude after flying into the propeller slipstream of a B5 (Northrop 8A-1) while simulating a stern attack.

39

CR.42 2563 (construction number 1003) of F 9's 1. *divisionen*, Kiruna, May 1942

Aircraft 2563 displays 1.*divisionen's* red wheel spats and the devil insignia introduced in early 1942. This aircraft was entered on the civilian register in July 1945 as SE-AOU and intended for use as a target tug. Its civilian career was to be short-lived, however, as the fighter was removed from the register in October 1946.

40

CR.42 (serial and construction numbers unknown) of F 9's 2.*divisionen*, Ånnsjön, February 1944

In the winter of 1944, 2.*divisionen's* F 9 transferred to Ånnsjön in the county of Jämtland. During a stop at F 4 Östersund, the fighter's wheels were exchanged for skis. The wheel spats are not fitted here, as they had to be modified when skies were attached.

BIBLIOGRAPHY

Becze, Csaba, *'Kör ász' Egy vadászrepülö század története 1936-1941.* Puedlo Kiadó, 2007

Bernád, Dénes, Dmitriy Karlenko and Jean-Louis Roba, *From Barbarossa to Odessa: Volumes 1 and 2.* Ian Allan Publishing Ltd, 2007-08

Brioschi, Angelo and Ali E Colori, *No 1 Fiat CR.42.* La Bancarella Aeronautica, 1999

Forslund, Mikael, *J11 Fiat CR 42.* Mikael Forslund Produktion, 2001

Cull, Brian with Don Minterne, *Hurricanes over Tobruk.* Grub Street, 1999

Gunby, David and Pelham Temple, *RAF Bomber Losses in the Middle East and Mediterranean, Volume 1.* Midland, 2006

Gustavsson, Håkan and Ludovico Slongo, *Desert Prelude, the Air War in North Africa 1940-41*

Malizia, Nicola, *Il FIAT CR 42 un mito che non muore.* Ateneo e Bizzarri, 1977

Shores, Christopher and Brian Cull with Nicola Malizia, *Air War for Yugoslavia, Greece and Crete 1940-41.* Grub Street, 1987

Shores, Christopher and Brian Cull with Nicola Malizia, *Malta: The Hurricane Years 1940-41.* Grub Street, 1987

Shores, Christopher and Corrado Ricci, *La Guerra Aerea in Africa Orientale 1940-41.* Mucchi, 1980

Taghon, Peter, *L'Aéronautique Militaire Belge en Mai-Juin 1940.* Éditions Lela Presse, 2006

INDEX

References to illustrations are shown in **bold**. Plates are shown with page and caption locators in brackets.